The Missing Piece

Coping with Grief

Compiled by Kate Batten

For permission requests, write to the publisher, addressed at the address below.

Mrs. Kate Batten

Email: katebatten1@gmail.com

SEATHORNE WALK, BRIDLINGTON,
EAST YORKSHIRE, ENGLAND, YO16 7QP

The Missing Piece

Book and cover design by Kate Batten
Edited by Kate Batten & Eileen Grubba
www.EileenGrubba.com
Formatted by: Kate Batten
ISBN: 9798551426684

In Loving Memory of David

I will never get to hold you,
or kiss your little head,
or ever watch you sleeping
soundly in your bed.

I can't count your tiny fingers,
or even your dinky toes
I won't see your smile,
or your cute little button nose.

4 years today was the day

you would have arrived.

However, God had plans which

Did not include you being alive.

I know you are above my head in heaven,
Where there are no tears.

The Missing Piece Coping with Grief

No hate, no pain and even no fears.

Today is the day I share with

the world your adorable face.

So that they can see your

adorable beauty and grace.

I am sad you are not here right

now for us to hold today.

However, I know I will hold

you in our arms in heaven one day.

Never a day passes without

me thinking of you.

You are always in

my thoughts in every action I do.

I will see you again,

but not yet cos it is too soon.

Nanna needs to stay here longer on Earth,

to help people shoot amongst the stars,

the sun, and the moon.

With love forever, Nana

Table of Contents

Appreciation

Rosie, David, and Hayden, until you three grandchildren came into my life, I did not realize how important it was to leave a legacy for generations to come. You moved me, changed me, and shaped me to become the grandma I am today.

David, it is heartbreaking that you passed-away so soon and that I will never see you grow up. I know you are watching over your nanna from heaven and one day we will meet again to catch up on all those missed hugs and kisses.

George, welcome to the family, it is a pleasure to have you, my bonus grandson!

I Love You!

Introduction

Grief is an emotion, a sad feeling that the whole of humanity can connect with. We can all agree that at some stage in our lives we have lost somebody we loved, or somebody close to us. We can all understand that deep sadness that grief leaves behind and agree that we feel shocked, disbelief and sadness. A place that was once filled with love, laughter, and life from a physical being, is now just an empty space that echoes the silence of the person you cared about so dearly.

Even though we all deal with the emotion of grief differently, there is still no denying that grief is extremely painful to feel and experience. Grief is something that stays with us forever. It never goes away, and it only changes form. We hear the common statements like: "I am so sorry for your loss" and "With time it will get easier I promise". Yet, the question still remains, does it really become easier? Do we ever really "get over" the loss of somebody?

The sentences spoken by others barely touch you or comfort you when you are in that zone of complete numbness, shock, and disbelief. In fact, in some cases you do not hear them at all, and as your life suddenly plunges into a reality that you really do not want to live in. This is when your brain goes into overdrive while it tries to wrap itself around what just happened. This is a way of your mind helping to protect your body from feeling the force of the shock by numbing you to a place that feels unnormal.

I wanted to fetch the subject of grief forward in The Missing Piece book series because I knew it was time, and I was ready to address this subject. It has been a subject I have lived with and experienced. I also wanted to share it so that people could stand with me knowing and never feeling they are alone in this world.

One cold November morning in 2016, my life changed forever when we lost our first grandson David. He died at birth and the experience shocked me and my family members to the core of our soul. It felt like I had all the life sucked out of me at that very moment in time. As I sat in a private hospital suite with my daughter, I held his tiny body wrapped in a blood-stained white towel. I was holding my screaming adult daughter in one arm and her dead son in my other. It was like experiencing a nightmare moment that you only watch in movies. I prayed so hard in that moment for him to move, to make a little squeaking noise like babies do, anything! I just prayed for any form of movement!! I even begged to God out loud "Please God anything!" But unfortunately, nothing came, and he remained still in my arms.

He was gone, and we had to accept it.

That afternoon me and my husband drove home in silence, numb, shocked and disbelief of how I had just spent my day. That afternoon turned into night and I couldn't sleep. I remember sitting in my office just staring out the window, feeling as if my heart had been ripped out my chest as I watched the clock strike 4 am and the sun started to rise to a new day.

It was suddenly in that moment at 4 am I decided I would write about how I was feeling and what had just happened in the past 24 hours. I pulled my keyboard towards me and started writing and could not stop writing for 15 days after David's death. I remember that after every 10 minutes of typing I would have to stop to dry off the tears from my keyboard, because it was soaked with the number of tears I had cried. I hunched over the keyboard wailing to the point my chest, back and heart ached so much, but still I carried on writing.

This was my grief transcending through my entire body. I was feeling it and now I was transferring it on to paper to help me deal with my emotions. I wanted to somehow to document it so that I could go back to it one day and maybe publish it to inspire others. 4 years later and here we are.

The Missing Piece: Coping with Grief is one of the hardest books I have ever had to write and place together. I cried many tears going back through my own story, as well as reading the powerful, moving experiences of our contributors. I hope that by reading this book, it really inspires you to appreciate and celebrate life more. To not take things so seriously and to let fun and laughter be the most important part of life. Plus, I hope it inspires you to make great memories that can be treasured forever. The truth is none of us know how much time we really do have on this planet and the only person with them answers is God Himself. It is only when we pass on to be greeted by Him is when we learn and understand why.

Welcome to The Missing Piece: Coping with Grief. I hope you enjoy the book. It is a blessing to share this book with the other amazing authors around the world who I invited to share their own experiences.

God Bless,

Kate x

Founder and publisher of The Missing Piece book series.

Kate Batten

Kate is the publisher and creator of the international best-selling book series The Missing Piece , Kate has helped over 500 authors hit the Amazon best sellers list and helped teach them to build extremely successful businesses through the power of publishing. Kate has worked with Hollywood TV personalities and award-winning film directors to help lead global projects to success. As a loving wife to Matthew, mother of 2 adult children and 3 grandchildren, Kate leads with a passionate desire to see people shine brightly at their best in everything they do.

Follow Kate on Instagram: @kate_batten

Email Kate: katebatten1@gmail.com

Chapter 1

Mums Fix Everything, Right?

By Kate Batten

Mums, we fix everything! Right? Well, at least that is what I thought.

For the past 20 years of my life as a parent, that is all I have been doing. The statements that all moms know so well: "Mum I need you to fix this, it's not working", "Mum how do I make this happen?", "Mum what do I do with this?", "Mum what am I supposed to do now?".

If you are a parent, like me, then you know them questions only too well from your children and you have adopted that role of mom, the "fixer". Well, I wish I could have fixed what happened to my daughter on that fateful day, but that was impossible. Nothing I could do would have fixed the situation we were in, and I felt completely useless.

I received a call at 6:30am yesterday morning to tell me my daughter's waters had broken, and that she was on her way to the hospital to give birth to her son. So, I sprang into mom fixer mode and started packing her hospital bag. We were so unorganized and not expecting this because she was only 27 weeks into her pregnancy, and this was majorly unexpected.

I started to rush around like a headless chicken fixing the hospital bag, cancelling all meetings that day and calling my husband back from work. As soon as my husband arrived home, we chucked everything in the car and headed straight to the hospital. I tried frantically to get in touch with my daughter on the way to the hospital and rang her mobile around 20 times, but she was not answering. Twenty minutes later, she called me to say she had delivered the baby, and it was not looking good.

At this moment in time, I was only 10 minutes away from the hospital, and now in shock has the tears started streaming down my cheeks. I needed to get there soon as possible. We pulled up into the hospital car park, I grabbed the bag out the trunk of the car, and my mobile phone rang again. It was my daughter Emily, in floods of tears, trying to speak between her sobs. "Mom he's gone. He's gone." She was trying to tell me the best she could that her baby had passed away. At that moment, I could not breathe. I felt like somebody had punched me in the stomach. I lost my balance for a moment and had to regain my stance on two legs, my mind whirling. All I could think was "Now, how the fuck am I supposed to fix this?" With tears streaming down my face I grabbed the hospital bag and ran to the special care baby unit. When we arrived at the desk, we were guided to a side room called the "Snow Drop" suite. The midwife could have been talking to me in French for all I know. My shocked brain just couldn't take in what she was saying and the only words I remembered her saying was "I am so sorry for your loss" the rest was a blur……..

Somehow, I moved into the Snow Drop suite with an urgency to hold my child because right now, I knew she would need her mother. I sat down on the sofa in the suite and waited for what seemed like 5 hours, though it was only ten minutes.

My heart leapt out my chest as the double doors swung open and the midwives pushed Emily's hospital bed into the room. I turned my head back to the door and there stood in the door frame was Mark, Emily's partner, holding his tiny son, wrapped in a white towel. Mark sat next to me, holding his son, and cried his heart out. I held Mark and told him how sorry I was as I looked down at the little bundle he was holding. He passed me the bundle and I held him in my arms. He was still warm, and he was the most beautiful thing I had ever laid eyes on.

His head was slightly tilted to the side and his mouth was open. For me, trying to get my mind to understand he was not alive was challenging. Every ounce of me hoped and prayed for a tiny noise, or movement, but nothing. He remained still in my arms and did not move. My tears fell from my cheeks onto his little pink forehead. I passed him to my husband, and walked over to the bed and sat next to Emily, and hugged her and told her how sorry I was. She looked at me and said "Sorry for what mum? You have no need to be sorry". I grabbed hold of her and held her so tightly, to let her know her mother was there to support her through this.

The rest of the morning was spent gathering footprints, handprints, and a lock of hair from David. I offered to wash him and dress him for his photo's to be taken. His tiny body was stuck to the white towel he had been wrapped in after birth and I had to peel the towel ever so gently away from his delicate skin, careful not to tear it. I washed him down to clean all the blood off his skin. I washed him from the top of his neck to the bottom of his dinky toes. He had such long legs, big hands, and big feet, as do all the boys in our family. His little tiny legs had started to turn black from no circulation or heartbeat in his little body. He also had a little bruise on his nose and chest where the nurses had tried to resuscitate him for over 30 minutes.

I dressed him in a little white vest, and wrapped him back up in his blanket, and lifted him up to my face to get a better look at him. I wanted to make sure that if this was the first time, and only time, I was going to see my grandson, then I needed to take in every detail of his face while I had the chance. I kissed his little cheek and felt the coldness of his skin against my lips. Now, it was becoming more real that he was dead by the temperature of his skin.

I placed him back in my daughter's arms and the vicar arrived to baptize him. We had a lovely little ceremony in the Snow Drop suite, He was blessed right there so that his soul was released to heaven, to rest in the arms of Jesus until we meet him again. I thanked the vicar for the lovely ceremony, and he looked at me and said: "I am so sorry for your loss. There are no words to console your pain right now". I looked at him with my tear stained face and said, "Mum's usually fix everything. This is something I cannot fix", the vicar looked at me and said, "I know. God bless you and your family". I shook his hand and thanked him for baptizing David, and he left the room.

I spent the next few hours with my grandson David, holding him, holding my own child, who was crying because she had lost her son. What I was experiencing in that moment was like a living hell that I would not have wished upon my worst enemy. We then said our goodbyes forever and I took some photos of him along with some foot and handprints. I kissed my daughter goodbye and knew it was now her time to spend some alone time with him until she decided she was ready to say goodbye for good. Myself and my husband drove home that afternoon in a state of shock, disbelief, and numbness of the situation we had just experienced. We said nothing. We could not think of anything to say, and just remained shocked. What had just happened? Was this even real?

Yes, it was real, and I was dreading the end of the numb feeling because I knew once that numb feeling had gone, then the pain that would hit me would feel like my heart was broken in two. The afternoon blurred into night, and I still sat in shock, staring into silence.

Would tomorrow feel any better than it does today? …

All I could do is hope.

Day 2:

Acceptance?

Acceptance, it is such an easy word to say, but it is the hardest thing you must do. This is the part in your life where you must take responsibility for your reality and see the situation for what it is and how it is.

However, even though you are seeing the reality of the situation, accepting that it has happened, and seeing it for what it is, you should never see it worse than it is. Even though you are going through your own private hell, you must still remember that each day the world keeps turning and life keeps moving.

You must also understand that no matter how much pain you are feeling there is still others that need you. to guide them. Especially if you have people who look to you for inspiration and need to be led, and most importantly a grandmother to another grandchild.

19

Throughout the journey of leadership, I learned that you must learn to separate yourself sometimes from what is going on around you to keep focused on, so things can keep moving forward. I cannot just let go and let other people's futures crumble by saying, "fuck this" and walk away.

So, even if it is for a few hours, 45 minutes or even ten minutes of the day, I still had work to do and a team to lead in the right direction of where they needed to be, to help make our clients dreams become reality. I will not lie, it has taken every ounce of mental strength I have daily to keep one leadership shoe on, support my daughter through the death of her son, and start to help plan an infant's funeral.

It is extremely painful to lay myself bare in front of you and to share the painful story of events that happened less than 48 hours ago. However, like most writers experience, it can be amazing therapy and release of the feelings that I am feeling, this is so they are not locked up inside driving me insane. It is also a great way for you and me to connect on a personal level. It can also help to lift the lid so that you can see even though someone can succeed and be creative in many ways, it makes no shitting bit of difference on the human side. Shit still happens in my world, and if any leader describes their life as perfect, then they are talking out of their arse! Leadership is HARD, and a TOUGH road, and it is not for everyone!

Hence, the reason why only few actual make it.

There is two different types of people: leaders, and followers. I was created for the leading part and in every situation, no matter in personal life or business, I lead the rest of the group. Sometimes days are tough and some days it is mega tough, but the overall outcome is priceless. I slipped into them leadership shoes for 30 minutes before the sun came up, in order to keep all projects on track and, keep the client's dreams on the road to reality.

Now, as I sit here and watch the sunrise on a new day, on entering the 3rd day of loss in our family. I have learned to accept the situation that David is gone. He is not alive, and we will never see him grow up. My daughter has also started to accept that she now needs to plan a funeral and take her first steps to call the funeral director. Before this happened, I could not even begin to understand how somebody feels when they lose a child, and now we are in it and living that insane reality that makes no sense at all. I know one day, all of this will make sense of why it has happened, and the pieces of God's plan will form sensibility.

Until then, all I know is that writing about it daily and sharing it one day will really help others, and it stops me going insane. I know one day these words will inspire many others experiencing grief themselves.

Day 4:

Release

Release, ready to let go, allowing one's self to leave.

This word relates to yesterday evening when my daughter discharged herself from the hospital. she had spent just over 48 hours with David in the Snow Drop suite. He laid beside her in a special cooler bed that filters cold air through its mattress to help keep his little body cool, so that he wouldn't deteriorate so rapidly, and Emily could spend more time with him.

She said her last goodbyes to David and left the hospital at 7pm, Matthew (my husband) took her home to begin her first night without her baby. Today will be the day she stumbles one foot in front of the other to start his funeral arrangements. Even though she is hurting right now and in a place that not many of us could even begin to comprehend, she is doing amazing and showing great strength of acceptance and knowing the next steps she must take.

As the sun rises on another day of this week, there is a knowing in my mind what the next steps are and how this whole experience can be turned into something good to help others. After David's birth/death, we were placed into a side room called the Snow Drop suite which had been designed and created by a charity called 4Louis. This charity had helped raised the money for this special private hospital suite, which is especially designed for parents experiencing stillbirths. Not only have they helped raise over £65,000 ($808,43.75) for each of these suites to be built, but they present the parents with a gift box full of ways to collect memories from their child. 4Louis aim to provide hospitals with memory boxes free of charge so they can be given to bereaved parents who suffer the trauma of stillbirth or neonatal death. Each box contains a clay impression kit for hand and feet imprints, teddy bears and an Angel, which signifies a sleeping baby, and more.

The charity supply over 200 hospitals in the UK with these memory boxes and donate all of it free of charge They raise the money to help make this happen in all kinds of ways. The founders of the charity, Kirsty McGurrell and her partner Michael, lost their own son in 2009. They started the charity based on their own experience of having to share a labor ward with other new mums after losing their own child, and not having the things they needed to hand to cherish them memories forever.

With over 3,500 stillbirths happening every year in the UK alone, you could only imagine how many that is worldwide?

How many mothers must stay on labor wards while listening to crying babies, when she has just lost her own? How many mothers have nothing to take home with them after the death of their babies? How many mother's struggle to dress their babies after still birth, like we did with David? Maybe this is the light peeking out from the journey of all this and me helping in this area? Who knows. We will see where that journey takes us. Right now, we are still only a few days into this painful week and we still have a lot to muddle through before we even consider the next huge step of turning our lemons into lemonade.

The support from people has been amazing and thank you for all those amazing messages. Letting others know what we are going through can fetch us closer together and on a deeper level of understanding that we are all in fact human, and shit does happen.

It is how you rise from that sadness that really determines the human being that you are and the purpose of the inspiration that you leave behind or place upon people. Giving them just a mustard seed of hope from your own strength can really help them too. Like I said yesterday, it is all tiny steps to healing each day. Each day the dark cloud above my head lifts ever so slightly, just a tiny amount. Enough for me to stumble forward another step.

Last night while I was sleeping, I heard a tiny voice shout out "Don't give up nana, don't give up" I knew instantly is was my little angel in heaven telling me to stay strong and carry on. So that is what I will do. It is all I can do. It is all the comfort I have knowing that this was God's plan all along.

Day 5:

Little by Little

Gradually, slowly, step by step, progressively, bit by bit is basically the journey we must take now. Healing is a progress, and it takes time, and it cannot be rushed.

We all have different ways of dealing with things and we all have different ways of coping with our grief. Each day for me the cloud lifts just that tiny bit more and I can think clearer each day. Emily is accepting a little more each day that her son is never coming back, but she is also accepting that he is always with her no matter what. She has started to plan how she would like David's service to look, and Emily being the rebel she is (no idea where she gets that from?) is not wanting it ordinary. She wants it colorful and she has asked all guests to wear some form of metallic blue and she has asked the men in our family to wear bright blue ties.

Today the birth and death of David was registered, and Emily has gone back to the hospital to hand in David's death certificate for them to release his tiny body to the funeral home. From here Emily can start to plan his funeral, set a date to lay him to rest and choose the little white coffin she wishes to lay David to rest in. It has only been 5 days since he died, and it already feels like this week has dragged on for 5 years. I am slowly getting back into work and taking on light duties. However, all the heavy stuff like really being in the public eye, interviews, video, consultation calls will have to wait for when I am ready because.

1) I look like shit.

2) I feel like shit.

3) I am doing it on my terms nobody else's.

and 4) Did I mention I look like shit?

One thing that does remain in this crap time is mine and Emily's sense of humor. We are picking one another up each day and making each other smile. Just to lift that sorrow even for 5 minutes keeps us in touch with knowing we can still laugh even in hard testing times. I have no idea where these daily journal notes will lead and one day? They may end up in a book who knows.

What I do know is it captures everything I am feeling and going through and keeping a record of our journey of loss.

I keep a deck of Doreen Virtue Angel cards on my desk and I pull one out most days. Yesterday I pulled the card "Blessing in Disguise" of which has come up many times on my life journey and usually does when I have experienced painful moments.

I wrote yesterday about knowing this was all for a bigger reason that we could not yet see, and that David's death was not for nothing. We must keep our feet moving and keep pushing one foot in front of the other and eventually all this crazy shit will make sense, even the reason behind why I felt the urge to write every day.

Here is to another sunrise, and another new day....

Day 6:

Guilt I am not owning you!

Guilt is something we all hang on to when something major traumatic happens. We go through the self-sabotage mode of blaming ourselves and we feel by blaming ourselves it will give some form of explanation to why it happened.

Well, I refuse to blame myself or feel any guilt for David's death. I refuse my daughter to blame herself too. If we rewind 6 years before I was a therapist, you bet I would have travelled down the route of self-blame and replayed 1,000 different scenarios in my head of how this was all my fault and what I could have done differently to stop it from happening.

What a difference 6-years and a different mindset can make. So, guilt guess what? Guilt, I am not owning you! This experience was no fault of anyone, and it was God's will. He took David to be back at His side because it is a lead to something more amazing and we have yet to learn and understand what. So, until that day I will keep running with the mindset that I have which is far away from the feeling and emotion of self-blame.

One lady messaged me yesterday and said:

"You're an amazing soul Kate! I want to send my condolences to you and your family. I am completely devastated by your family's loss. I know the little guy is still with you guys. In spirit! Sending so much love!!! I am so inspired by your strength. You continued to work forward for the I Rise project even during the difficult time in your life. You're a true inspiration, I am just so glad that you and I have crossed paths!!"

-Kristie Knights

What else did I have? It's either keep inspiring others and share this heartbreaking journey with you, or I stare at the wall all day and sit in silence while the grief rips me apart inside while pretending to the outside world my life is great. I am not a robot, and I cannot lie or deny what am going through. So, I would rather share it and together we can unite through the sorrow as well as the good.

I also learned yesterday that my little sister will not even get out of bed each morning until she has read my daily post. Like I mentioned yesterday, when I said I had such an urge to write the day after David passed away, and just couldn't stop and continued to share the feelings with the words of meaning that popped into my head daily. So many people can stay in a dark place of loss for years. I refuse to do that! David's very short time on this planet was for a reason and that will be celebrated rather than mourned. It will take time, but as a family we will find joy again and get through the painful loss of him, and we WILL turn this into something inspirational. So that when we do eventually all reunite in heaven again, he can be so proud of his nana and give me a big hug.

Please do not feel sadness for me, feel love and celebrate the fact the short time with David was not for nothing. It was for something bigger than we cannot yet see. Who knows? We could be all coming together to make an impact in the world in his memory. Thank you to those for sharing this journey with me and thank you for spreading David's memory across the world by sharing my posts.

P. S) Guilt I am not owning you!

Day 7:

Choice

Choice is exactly what life is and the emotions we feel…

We can choose to feel miserable and choose to be a victim and cry all day and say, "You don't understand what I am going through", blah blah blah. Or we can get up off our backsides and decide how we are going to make a crap time like this somehow better? I choose to take responsibility for life and choose not to be miserable. I choose not to hide behind any excuse or have any excuse to keep me stuck in a dark place. The darkness will suck you in if you let it!

It will take you hostage if you allow it and it will not let you back out in a hurry. Which is why you need to take a good firm grip of your choices and choose to move forward. Even if it is just a tip toe step forward every day. Each time you move forward it is another inch away from the darkness into the lighter side of emotion. I will not deny taking that choice of stepping away from darkness is mentally draining and takes a heck of a lot of focus. More focus than writing a book or leading the big projects I do. But in the end, it is either practically limping to the light, or tumbling into darkness.

So, here is me CHOOSING to keep focused on this Sunday morning and end this dreadful week of loss, pain, sadness, and death by using all my focus and energy limping towards the light.

The darkness will never win this one.

Day 8

Alone...

There is always that thought that comes into your head a few times even when you do not want it to. That is the "alone" thought and vision. You know for a small moment that your ego wants to bash your brain with a negative thought of how alone David is and how his tiny body is stuck on a cold slab in the hospital morgue. I will not lie, that thought went through my head when the funeral director said he could not talk to Emily until Monday when she rang them on the Saturday.

I had to fight back that negative thought with the positive thought that his soul is never alone because it is in heaven and that is where he is in great care. Where he is surrounded by many other of our family members, the angels, God, and Jesus. So alone does not even come close to it and he is far from alone. This is again where thought control comes in and you change the direction of your thought pattern to feel better because again, it is all by choice. Like I mentioned yesterday, I would rather keep limping towards the light then letting the darkness take me hostage.

Emily is doing well, and she left the house on Friday afternoon and went to do some shopping. It was nice to see her up, dressed and out the door for the first time since she left the hospital. I will not deny it was strange to see her today without her pregnancy belly because she was rather big for 27 weeks. However, like every part of this journey, we must slowly get used to the cold fact that David is no longer with us. Not an hour passes that I don't think about him and I cannot tell you how many times I have picked up my phone to look at his photo of him in his little blue hat and wrapped in his blanket. It really places the true meaning of how precious life is into perspective and how lucky I am to have one healthy and amazing grandchild who is alive and healthy.

The gift of life is the most precious gift of all and if there is one thing this journey has taught me is cherish every second of you and your family's life.

Day 9:

The Date is Set ...

Think of a rollercoaster track and how the cart slowly is pulled up the track. As the chain pulls the cart up your nerves jump in the pit of your stomach because you know when you get to the top you will dip so fast that it will feel like your stomach will pop out your mouth. My emotions over the past week have resembled the feelings you have when you ride that rollercoaster track. Just when you think everything is looking a little brighter and your mood is lifting, there is a major dip in the track. Yesterday I was doing so well until towards late afternoon when the funeral date was announced.

Boom! back into the dip of reality of loss and grief.

The dread of knowing I must see a tiny white coffin placed in the ground on Friday really is gut wrenching. I have 3 days to somehow gather the strength, courage and will to get through that day. I must be the strengthen tower that my girl needs her mum to be. All I can do is look up to the heavens and ask God to send me the strength I need and keep focusing on me limping towards that light.

Today's duties that matter are ordering flowers, posting a signed copy of one of my books, sending my latest book to the printers, and praying to God for strength....

Please God give me strength.

Day 10

Flowers....

Yesterday was another huge dip in that rollercoaster track again when I had to sit and look through a funeral flower catalogue. Sitting there trying to get to grips that this was really happening and what color flowers should I have? It sucked big time! Well, let me be completely honest with you and tell you it sucked balls!

Your mind races in every direction and trying to focus on the job at hand and it is really hard work. Your mind wants to escape the horror and not actually take in what you are buying these flowers for, so your mind wonders into places that have fuck all to do with ordering the flowers. After an hour of mind-numbing searching and looking at the same 20 images repeatedly I finally ordered a basket of blue and white carnations that comes with a blue teddy and a balloon. Then the dip came *again* and left me feeling like shit.... *Again!* Hello grief my old friend, thanks for coming to visit to me to remind me of how much pain I am in, and now please can I just order these bloody flowers?

I extended my finger and pushed the buttons on my keyboard to spell out on my Facebook status: *The flowers are ordered, and the funeral is on Friday. I cannot express how much this sucks balls right now! God give me the bloody strength to get through it!*

I thought "fuck this" and just hit the post button, why? Because if I were to lie to you and not show you the raw truth what kind of leader would that make me? It would make me a liar! One that only shows her following that life is amazing when you are successful, and no shit happens to you...**FALSE!** It does not matter how many books you have on the best sellers list, or how much a person has achieved. When it boils down to it, we are all human and we all must deal with what life throws at us. So, I am not going to lie about it, and neither am I going to hide it.

I am like any other human being that is riding the rollercoaster of emotion of losing a grandchild. I still must get up every morning and run a business and keep the projects I lead running. I have my moments where I dip and then get back up and keep going. I know that eventually, the dipping will become less, and time will heal.

However, right now I am not hiding from my true reality. Take the analogy of flowers for instance, when flowers have grown, they needed to push through the dirt to be bathed in sunlight.

I know there is sunlight at the end, and right now am just pushing my way through the cold hard dirt. I do not know how long it will be before I reach the sun light, but here is to me pushing!

Day 11:

Preparation

Today across America people will be preparing for Thanksgiving. Families will be arriving, and the celebrating will begin. Today my day is full of preparation for family arriving and there is preparation happening in my own house too, but it is a far cry away from celebrating Thanksgiving.

We are preparing to say goodbye to my grandson David. Celebrating the little time, he had on this planet with us and laying his tiny body to rest tomorrow. My family will start arriving later today and preparation for the day begins. My blue jacket has arrived, and I hope (fingers and toes crossed) that the men's ties arrive today, or it will be a mad rush tomorrow morning to the supermarket to find 3 blue ties!

Fingers crossed that I do not have to dash around a supermarket in the morning.

Day 12:

Lanterns to heaven

Saturday was completely exhausting, and I could not even find the strength to do the grocery shopping. Every ounce of energy was used to get me and my family through the funeral on Friday and I needed two days of complete rest to recharge. On Friday morning at 11:20am the funeral car pulled up outside my daughter's home. Inside the black limousine laid the tiniest of white coffins I had ever seen in my life. David had his name engraved on a little silver plaque attached to the lid. We drove in complete silence to the church that day. There were no words of comfort that any of us could say in that moment in time.

My stomach churned when we approached the church gates, and the vicar was waiting for us outside along with all the other guests. It is like your stomach ties in complete knots because you know this is REALLY happening! The tiny coffin was carried out of the car and we all followed behind and went inside the church. The vicar presented David with a beautiful service and everything was how my daughter wanted it to be.

The next part, however, was going to be the hardest part. That was the part where we had to bury him. After the service we all walked back outside, and his little coffin was placed back into the funeral car and off we went to the cemetery. His grave was ready and prepared and was such a tiny hole that looked like a rabbit had dug it.

The vicar carried on the rest of the ceremony, blessed David's grave and we finally laid his tiny body to rest. As he was lowered into the grave, a flock of birds flew above our heads and moved in such a beautiful way. It was like a sign from God to let us know he was right with us at that very moment. People placed roses and teddy bears inside his grave and we all said our final painful goodbyes before leaving David in his final resting place.

The full service was so beautiful, and the vicar was amazing. He even offered to help Emily with David's headstone in 6-months' time, when the ground settles, he wants to help her pay for it, have it chosen and help lay it in place.

I stood at the side of David's grave with my baby (Emily) in my arms and waited for her to be ready and leave. I did not mind if it took hours, I was prepared to wait with her until she was ready to walk away from that hole. Eventually she was ready, and she blew a big kiss to her son and said goodbye.

We all climbed back into the funeral car and set off to the after ceremony. Where we all stayed together as a family until the sky turned dark. Just as the night sky turned dark, we drove to the top of the white cliffs and lit our Chinese lanterns and sent them up to heaven. We watched them fly over the sea and go up and up towards the stars and straight to heaven. The whole day was such a beautiful way to say goodbye to David. I could not have asked for a better way to do it.

I praise God for keeping David at His side until we meet again.

Day 13:

Abnormal

Abnormal is something that is on the complete opposite spectrum of normal, so far from normal that you could not even quite grasp the reality of it, right?

Well, this is where we are right now, living a life of abnormality that has become the new normal. Instead of wrapping up gifts and placing them under the Christmas tree like other grandparents, we are discussing on how to make our grandson's grave a better resting place. Having discussions on how we can place a little fence and windmills around his grave to make it look better while we must wait 6 months before a headstone can be fitted.

This right here has become our new normal, only it is a normality that I would have never thought in a million years would be our reality.

However, it now is our reality, and we must begin to understand this abnormal living as normal as possible. That is quite a deep thought, right? But I would not know how else to think because my daily work is to think deep. My daily work is to create solutions for people, to make them see a different alternate way of mindset so they can achieve what they first thought was impossible. So, maybe this does need the deepness of thought, maybe it does need to be focused upon so that those who have experienced losing a loved one can begin to understand that we must make an abnormal reality or own way of normality.

We will have to consider things that not every day normal parents/grandparents with healthy children have never the need to consider. Birthdays and Christmases are no longer a decision of "What can I get him this year?", instead, it's replaced with "How can I make his resting place more beautiful?".

Which is making normal from an abnormal reality.

Day 14:

The Shift

A shift happens when you have experienced something so big that it completely transforms the way you do things. It is bizarre how the loss of David has completely shifted me in many ways and not just in life but in business too. You see, I did use to have little room for excuse making from people, now I have minus zero tolerance for it and will not accept any excuses from nobody. It is far from having a hardened heart or grieve causing this, because that is so far from the truth.

The shift has happened because even though I was in my darkest times last week, I STILL stuck to commitments to help make people's dreams become reality. I STILL stuck to the projects I was leading and kept my team moving to make our client's books go to print. So, when you STILL stick to your commitments, even when you feel like you don't want to, it begins to strength something inside of you that will not tolerate what it used too. It completely shifts things in business and makes you see everything from a different light and it also shifts things in your family too. It makes you realize where you have gone wrong in not spending as much time as you could have with siblings. It shifts the pattern of how you will change things in future and travel to see them more instead of letting life take over and not seeing them for 3-5 years at a time.

Life is a gift and so precious, yet we take it for granted and sometimes we just expect that people will be around forever. Well, that is very untrue, and life can be snapped away in an instant, which this family learned in a big way only days ago. We have now learned not to leave things so long next time and not to let "life in general" keep us apart. It all creates a shift pattern that will now change the course of how we do things, how we show up for one another, and how much effort we truly place into appreciating one another. Take my advice, do not let death be the course of you realizing how lucky you are to have an amazing family, realize it now and treasure it forever.

Yesterday is history, tomorrow is a mystery, and today is a gift that is why they call it the present!

Day 15

Getting There

Is the term "Getting there" used for when we want to tell somebody we are making progress? When somebody asks the question of "How are you doing?". That is all the words I can really reply with right now. "Am getting there". Getting there is better than zero progress at all, and it shows hope with steps in the right direction of healing.

Yesterday was the first Skype call I had taken since David's death. It felt strange to be slowly placing myself back in front of people when I have taken time out. Even though it was only one call you are still having to place yourself in front of the public again after a traumatic event. But it is all part of the "Getting there" process I suppose?

I must start to fetch normality back in, so I can move forward with my life and accept my grandson is gone. I have decided that by next Thursday I will be back fully with my work, but until then…

I am getting there…………………..

4 Years Later

Clarity

To read back through the diary I had written during the 15 days after losing my grandson David, was extremely hard work. I did not realize until now how much pain from the experience was still within me. I knew I had come to a time in my life where I was ready to make my experience of losing David public and publish it in a Missing Piece book, but I wasn't prepared to feel that it still hurts 4 years later after reading it. Each day after editing and formatting this book, the sad feeling of grief did pop up. I will not deny it, however now I embrace that feeling and I know that I will not be sad every day. I know I will smile again and that my grief just moves along with me.

Grief is real and it only ever changes form but never goes away. The feeling of emotion still pops and so does the prang of sadness that David is still not here. The question on my mind as each of his birthday's pass is: What would he look like now? So much has happened since I wrote that diary, and I still have no idea why I only wrote for 15 days and never anymore after that?

I could not even remember half of what I had written, so reading back over it to place in this book was interesting. Especially, with how deep the thought pattern of my mind went and the showing of hope to find explanation into why my grandson died. Clarity is such a powerful thing in life and our minds will do everything they can to find the reasoning behind why something has happened to us.

When we receive that clarity, we can start to fill in the holes that left us feeling so empty for so long. I knew in the mist of my grief at the time of David's death that something would come from the who painful situation, yet I could not yet see what it was? Now I know the why. Experiencing the loss of David really opened my eyes to how much help is needed to dress babies after they have died. The whole experience taught me how much of a struggle it was for the nurses to find David something to wear, because it is something that is not expected by the parents, nor is it planned for by the hospital. Here was something where I could turn my grief into something useful to help others and turn our own tragedy into something wonderful by easing the pain of others in the same situation.

In 2017 I launched David's Little Angels which is a non-profit campaign that transforms donated wedding gowns into baby angel gowns. The wedding gowns donated to my cause come from amazing women from across the world who contact me to send me their used wedding gowns.

I take the wedding gowns and transform them into beautifully decorated gowns and donate them to the hospital so that the pain stalking process of wondering what to dress a baby in after it's passing is taken care of. I do this so the parents can concentrate fully on spending what little time they have with their little angels before they have to say goodbye for good. Plus, they never have to worry about pulling a towel from the babies' delicate skin and tearing it. After the donated wedding gowns are transformed to angel gowns, I then deliver them to the local hospital where David was born and donate them to The Snow Drop Suite to help dress 100 baby angels a year.

When I first set up David's Little Angels I did not even know how to sow. I just knew in my heart that this was something I had to do, so I set about watching 3 thousand hours of YouTube videos (or it felt like 3 thousand hours anyway). I invested in a sowing machine with a willing to learn. I placed the word out to the world through social media and the wedding dresses started to arrive at my home, this was it. This was my clarity! This is what I needed to be doing because God was fetching these dresses forward. It was His plan.

There was a reason behind this after all and it felt great to be able to channel my grief into a cause that would be helpful to others and give them hope that there is light at the end of the dark tunnel of loss. It would also take away the pain of the parents having nothing to dress their babies in after an unexpected stillbirth.

I want to end our time together in the book by sharing 5 helpful tips and advice with you that really helped me on my own journey of grief.

1. Write it out of you

One of the best therapies for me is to write out my traumatic experiences so that they are no longer swirling around in my head. I have done this with all my past experiences, including losing David. At the time it made no sense to me why I was writing; I just knew by placing it on paper or typing it up it was taking it out of my head and clearing the fog to allow me to see clearer.

2. Be patient with those around you

When David died nobody around me knew what to say, or what to do. This is a natural reaction from people, and it is something that you need to be patient with yourself. I felt the need to talk about David, yet the response I was getting from others was the sound of "crickets" which left me in a place of frustration and feeling like I was not being heard.

I was being heard, but people just did not know how to respond to our family losing a child. I could have made them situations a lot better by understanding their side and having a little more patience, rather than just been locked in my own pain and expecting them to know what to say and do. Not everybody has lost a child, a mother, a father etc... So, a little patience rather than expectancy of them knowing how you feel will help you in the long run.

3. Cry and let it all out

Never hold back your tears, and if you feel the need to cry then cry. If you feel the need to shout, scream or sink to your knees than do it. Embracing the grief is a step forward in accepting that they are gone. Without this we just bottle up our feelings and by doing that it could lead to major explosions or even emotional breakdowns which is not good. Allow yourself to feel your emotions and let it all out! You will feel so much better afterwards.

4. Channel your grief into something

Channelling your grief into something really helps fill the dark empty hole that remains inside your heart after the loss of someone. The more angel gowns I sow and create the more that dark hole deep down inside closes. It has fulfilment because I just created something that will easy the worry of grieving parent ever so slightly, of which when you are living in that experience the last thing you want to do is worry about finding something to dress your baby in.

I encourage you to channel your grief into helping those who have experienced the same as you, in a way that just eases their experience by a tiny amount. You may think why would I want to only ease their experience by a small amount? Because my darling, it fills your dark empty hole right up with compassion and love.

5. Keep their memory alive

By keeping their memory alive you are not losing sight of the fact they were a part of your life. The person you lost did exist and they are a part of your family tree, so keep their memory alive. A great way to do this is have framed pictures of your lost loved ones in your home, so that when people visit, or the next generation of your family ask, "Who is that?", you can then describe who they were and go on to share stories and experiences that you had with that person.

It is a great way to keep their memory alive and their legacy real in your present reality. Because when somebody dies it does not mean their work is finished, it can only live on through you by keeping their memory alive for them.

I have a photo of my grandmother on my laptop background wallpaper, and even though she passed over 10 years ago, my grandkids will always know their great grandmother was the inspiration in my life who made me who I am today.

So, keep their memory alive, always! 😊

The Missing Piece

Introducing

The Amazing Co-Authors

Adriane "Bella" Deithorn

Adriane Deithorn, MS has been a development professional for more than 18 years. Recognized as a leading expert in her field.

She has worked with a variety of organizations, from human services to the arts to higher education. Her specialties include Grant writing, strategic planning, nonprofit board development, special events, sponsorship procurement, event planning, sponsorship development, fundraising counsel, planned giving, development audits, policy development, writing for fundraising/marketing, board training, cultivation/solicitation planning, and nonprofit board development

Adriane has helped small and large nonprofits alike raise millions of dollars through capital campaigns, board development, events, telethons, annual fund campaigns, direct mail, major gift solicitations, and planned gift solicitations.

Nonprofit development can be complicated as well as difficult. Adriane's primary mission is to make nonprofit development simple and effortless. She helps you clear away the complexity and raise funds much more effectively. To achieve her mission, Adriane is continuously improving herself and her fundraising expertise.

Find out more at:

http://wishhopedreams.com/

Chapter 2

The Day I Lost My Mom!

By Adriane "Bella" Deithorn

It's been a little over 24 years since I lost my mom to cancer. When I say the words "I lost my mom" out loud, they still don't seem right. Today I still have a huge hole in my heart, which will never, ever go away.

When you lose anyone, it can be heart wrenching. However, losing a parent is an entirely different loss. It makes just getting up in the morning a challenge. It means that every time you see something that reminds you of them, you literally break down. Over the many years I have been without her, it gets easier, yes, but sometimes it triggers me to the point of tears.

The words "your mom died" will go through your head over and over again. I realized she would not be around to see me graduate from college, buy my first home, see my brother get married nor would she ever get the opportunity to be a grandmother. She wouldn't be around to celebrate 30 years of marriage with my father and she wouldn't be there to help me through the troubles most 21-year old's have along the way. I think of her every single day; she is the first thought on my mind the minute I wake up and she is the last thought before I lay my head down to go to sleep.

There are a million things that change and take on new meanings and shapes. There are a million words that suddenly don't seem so nice anymore. There are a million faces and things that don't bring comfort, like they used to.

I know time will help. But let's face it, it's been 24 years and it is still hard. This isn't my first loss, but it is the hardest. So here are a few things that happen when your mom dies, in case you wanted to know why your friend who lost her own mom opens up all the wounds again, or cries at a simple commercial.

You cry a lot, and at random times. I can't begin to tell you how many times I've seen a cute commercial and started sobbing hysterically. Maybe the character's mom was cheering them on at a game, or maybe she was just giving them a hug. Literally anything that shows another mom in it will have you crying.

Don't even get me started on walking around in public and seeing another mom with their child. That can be the worst! You may get closer to your dad. This isn't really a negative. When you lose your mom, you suddenly realize that you need your dad's support and strength more than ever. While he's grieving as well, there's something special about sharing this together and being able to reminisce as a pair. You realize that you start telling your dad about your day in the same way you used to tell your mom, in hopes that maybe things will feel normal. It doesn't, but it does help a little to know that someone still has your back, and you're not going into every situation alone.

My life, at times, seems like you're permanently wearing sunglasses, never the same brightness it was before. I don't know how to explain this to someone who hasn't lost a parent. Just trust me, nothing will have the same brightness after you lose your mom.

That brings me to my next point of contention and probably something that really used to bother me. People really expect you to be fine after about a week or two. If they aren't a part of the "I lost a parent" club, people expect you to be back to normal pretty fast. Once the shock and craziness of the funeral wears off, people will slowly start to forget about your pain and expect you to be normal again. It's normal to avoid people for a little while, I sure did. You will still be grieving. However please remind those who you love, how hard it is. Sometimes people are so focused on themselves, they forget how to be a real friend.

I tried to push through quickly and to be normal, I really did, but I failed miserably. Grief would slip out of me and I would find myself hysterically crying in the middle of the grocery store, the middle of a spinning class, the middle of walking or just sitting in my house. When I would go to my dad's, I felt like I should act like I was "fine". I didn't want him to think I was falling apart., unable to handle this alone or think that he needed to be around me constantly so he could see if I slipped into a depression. I held a lot of my sadness inside. It's hard to fully grieve, especially when you're a person that is outgoing, has a giant group of friends, and rarely if ever, cries in front of anyone. The other day I was making spaghetti sauce from scratch and for the life of me I could not remember her secret ingredient. Guess what happened? Yep, you bet, I began to sob and cry again. This is 24 years later, friends. It never really stops; you just learn to accept it. However, grieving this long after her death is still normal, but when it gets to be an issue is when it halts your life, daily.

This can be extremely frustrating, even today. You will become jealous and envious of everyone else who still has a mom. I found this to be true when my friends or family take her for granted. From this point forward, you shall never complain about your parent in front of me again. Because darling, you have no idea how lucky you are and how much I want to be in your shoes. Cherish them. Love them. Be thankful you have one more day with them. Believe me I have really made some of my friends mad when I have said these things. Actually, I have lost a couple, because I just "don't understand the circumstances".

Some of my final thoughts to those of you reading this. Make sure, if you still have one or both of your parents, tell them you love them as much as you can. Make sure you take the time to call them, at least weekly. Don't text or email, actually speak live. Facetime if you can, they love seeing you. If you live close to them, make time to see them in person. There will be NO ONE else in this world that you can count on like you can count on your mom and dad. Seek their advice, their wisdom. And please, whatever you do, don't take these moments for granted. You only have one mom and dad and when either of them are gone you'll wish you'd never said an ugly word to either of them your whole life.

Through the heartbreak, change, and devastation I have learned some key points that will help me and you, along with several others on the healing journey. I refer to them as "Bella's Best"!

1. Nothing lasts forever. Remember every time it rains, it stops raining. Every time you hurt; you heal. After darkness always comes light. Nothing lasts forever. We all might as well smile while we are still here.

2. Love is stronger than death. As weird as this may sound, my relationship with my mom continues on each and every day and will for the rest of my life. I always see pieces of her in myself every time I look in the mirror. When I do any type of charity work, I feel she is within me because this type of work she loved. She lives on through me, there is no doubt about it. When I hear mine and my mom's song "Wind Beneath My Wings" by Bette Midler, I feel as if we are together. Physical planes cannot separate love, no matter what.

3. It will forever be a part of who I am. I've met many people after losing my mom. It's almost as if I want to introduce myself as "Hi, I'm Adriane, I'm 45 years old, I'm a motherless daughter and I lost my mom to breast cancer." The question "So tell me about your parents?" is like nails on a chalk board. Those who truly know me and knew my mom, know pretty much every heartbreaking detail of the pain I've endured after losing her, but for those who I've recently met or have yet to meet have no idea. Losing my mom has reshaped who I am, how I see the world, and has changed my life forever.

4. Memories are gold. Memories, the most important thing to cherish. They flood through my mind all the time. The good memories are more so from before she was diagnosed with cancer. But I will literally NEVER forget the last few days of her life. We shared laughs, cries, and all different types of emotions but the memory I will be forever grateful for occurred just minutes before she died. I knew something was wrong, I knew the end was near. My heart began beating out of my chest, I grabbed her hand looked her right in the eyes and my last words to her were "I love you so much". She looked at me, squeezed my hand and she didn't have to say a word, I knew how much she loved me. In that moment I realized that I have received more love from her in my 21 years with her than most receive in a life time.

5. Some things will just always be out my control. Watching someone you love suffer, is one of the worst experiences you can imagine. All you can do is stick by their side, hold their hand, and try to make them smile

through the pain. It's a huge sense of helplessness and you want to take all the pain away for them, but some things will forever be out of your control. I fought endlessly to try to save my mom's life and I just couldn't, there was nothing more I could do but let her know how loved she was.

6. Music heals more than you can even imagine. Personally, I love music. I love songs with deep meanings. One song that makes me smile when I am feeling down is "What a Wonderful World" by Louis Armstrong. Whenever I hear it, it reminds me that my mom always saw the best in life, the best in people and truly lived her life.

7. Life is for the living, so live it. After a tremendous loss, many people go down the wrong road. For me, I threw myself into all positivity and doing things for me. I often find myself doing certain things and I think how unfair it is that my mom isn't here to enjoy the little pleasure that life brings. I also look at it as more a reason to go out and live. To this day, I do the things she loved to do; I do the things I love to do, more so now than ever. Life is just too damn short.

8. To the world you may be one person, but to one person you may be the world, remember that!

Eileen Grubba

Eileen Grubba is a lifetime *member of The Actors Studio with over 26 years of experience on the stage. She has worked on HBO's* Watchmen, *Netflix's* The Politician, *NBC's* Game of Silence, Sons of Anarchy, Criminal Minds, Bones, Fear The Walking Dead, CSI: Miami, The Mentalist, Hung, Cold Case, Nip/Tuck, The Closer, Monk, and many more.* She worked opposite Jessica Lange and Shirley MacLaine in *Wild Oats*, and with Emily Blunt in *The Five Year Engagement*. She has been nominated multiple times for Best Actress in Indie films, with three wins for Best Ensemble Cast in the female lead.

At age five, Eileen was paralyzed from the waist down from a spinal injury due to a vaccine. Doctors said she would never walk again, but she regained mobility through relentless persistence and many surgeries. She later beat cancer caused by radiation exposure during her medical battles.

Eileen is an accomplished actress, writer, public speaker, and producer with years of experience in casting. She has directed theater, films, and has been hired to write screenplays due to her ease with creating strong female characters. She is an advocate for the hiring of people with disabilities in film, television and advertising, and serves on the SAG/AFTRA National PWD Committee. A fighter all her life, Eileen refuses to give up her quest to create equal opportunity for people with disabilities, believing inclusion in entertainment will create a world of greater acceptance for all. #ALLin

Find out more at:

www.eileengrubba.com
Twitter: @EileenGrubba
Instagram: EileenGrubba
Facebook Page:

https://www.facebook.com/EileenGrubbaOfficialPage/

Chapter 3

Living with Grief

By Eileen Grubba

I thought we had time. I thought we had more time. It's one of the many things that race through the grieving mind as we try desperately to process the loss. You feel like it is going to break you. Your mind and entire body go into immense distress. How on earth are we going to get through this?

If we had known, what would we have done differently? I should have known. Lord knows, I have lost enough loved ones before. Profound losses, and never did we realize how fast they were going to happen. The most shocking one was my Mom. We were young, naïve, oblivious. She was always so healthy and strong. How was this even possible? No one dies this young! No one we knew had lost their mom! In disbelief, I prayed, I begged, I cried, I silently screamed into my pillow at night, and even offered to take her place. I couldn't accept that there was nothing I could do to stop this unfathomable outcome. On the day she left this world, I couldn't even catch my breath. In the weeks that followed, I couldn't figure out how to live with it, or even how to get through a day without paralyzing grief and emotional distress. One day I found myself lying on the floor, pounding my fists into the ground, sobbing uncontrollably. I couldn't accept that she was gone, and didn't know how to go on without my beautiful Mom. That day, I decided the only way to survive was to not allow myself to even think about her, especially her final weeks, because the thoughts were too painful. I remember how enormous the grief was that swallowed my father's mighty spirit. My own heart was so broken that I didn't really know how to help him, except to just *be there*. Be there when the crushing grief and reality of the loss dropped him to his knees. *Be there* and accept whatever he was going through, no matter how unpleasant it was. He said it was like half of him was ripped away, and he couldn't find it anywhere. Dad was diagnosed with cancer just a few months after she died. We were terrified of losing him too. It's too soon, God! Why? We had not even begun to accept, or come to terms with losing our mom, so how could we possibly endure losing Dad, too? It would destroy us. I begged God to just give us a few more years.

In six years, we lost seven relatives: mom, grandparents, uncles, a great aunt, and then Dad. I will never forget the agony my grandmother expressed when she saw her youngest son in a coma, at the end of his life. That guttural, painful moan from a mother losing her child has stayed with me all these years. This was the second son she lost in a few years. She died shortly after, the grief too much to bear. Her last child, our Auntie Ardelle, soon passed away from cancer too. My dad's entire family... *gone*.

Loss has become a regular part of my life. When I think of loss, so many horrible memories come to mind. I think of losing my ability to walk as a small child. A vaccine attacked my spinal cord and nearly killed me. Losing the use of my legs and half of my bodily functions was a huge life adjustment, to say the least. I've overcome a lot, but spent every year since dealing with the consequences. My mother gave me strength through it all, and wisdom that lasted my lifetime. Her words still come to me when I am facing another loss or challenge. Good thing, because I have since faced cancer myself and almost every other kind of loss. Loss of health, loss of abilities, loss of loved ones, loss of a marriage, a home, family, loss of unborn children, work, dreams, loss of hope, loss of faith. *SO MUCH LOSS.* Why does it keep coming and what are we supposed to do with it?

You would think we would get better at it, but here I am again, in this year of 2019, dealing with two more devastating losses that feel unbearable, unfair, unacceptable, unimaginable, and yet, what choice do we have but to grin and bear it? Each loss piles on top of the last, and the mountain gets bigger and heavier the longer we live. I have figured some things out along the way, learned a few tricks to get through, but it doesn't get any easier. I love just as much - perhaps even more - so therefore, every loss still brings with it immense grief. This year, I lost the most important person in my life: my *soulmate*.

I wake up every morning with sadness since he died. He was my best friend, my family, my partner-in-crime, my champion, my cheerleader, my mentor, my advisor, my business ally, my laughter, my release when life got too heavy. He had an amazing ability to calm my spirit. We could laugh at anything. We could talk about anything. We accepted each other, exactly as we were, unconditionally. That is so rare that I fear I may never feel that kind of connection again. He was the only person who really *knew* me, since my Mom. He knew my challenges. He knew my broken parts. He knew my spirit, my fire, my past, my dreams, and he loved ALL of it, all of ME. I knew him, his brilliant mind, his broken heart, his forgiving nature, his childlike spirit. His kindness warmed my soul. His laughter lit up my heart. His smile lit up the world around us. *How can I be expected to let all that go?* In an instant. Gone. He was a huge part of my life for 14 years, but still... I thought we had more time. Even as I write this, the tears flow. They never seem to stop. Even when I'm smiling, the tears are always there, just beneath the surface, waiting for a moment to escape. An image, a song, a place, a memory, anything that will give those tears the momentum to break free and soak my face and spirit again. Will I ever *not* be sitting on a river of tears? Will I ever feel happy again? Will I ever stop missing this kindred spirit who made me feel seen, heard, appreciated? Made me feel loved? Made me finally feel... *HOME*?

Two days after he died, I woke up and saw a vision. It was in my mind, although I was wide awake. I saw Carmen, smiling, laughing, with my Mom and Dad. My father was shaking Carmen's hand, with his left hand firmly placed on Carmen's shoulder. "Thank you for looking after my girl for a while", was what I heard, and suddenly this man's role in my life made a lot more sense. There was pure joy. Carmen was so proud, like he had accomplished something far greater than any award he may have received on this earth. Like everyone, he had disappointments about not accomplishing all he hoped for in his career, not winning the awards and accolades he worked so hard for, not being strong enough to really break free from the mistakes of his past. *But had he accomplished something far more important?* One only had to witness his memorial at The Actors Studio to feel the impact this man had on so many people. It makes perfect sense to me that he would be greatly rewarded in heaven for the countless lives he touched on earth. Carmen always admired and respected my Dad, and talked about him often, although he only knew him through my stories. He said he wanted to be like my Dad. So to have earned Dad's praises in the heavens would certainly have been a great reward for Carmen. Knowing he was now with my Mom and Dad was a great comfort to me.

Was that vision a message from heaven? Or was it something my mind conjured up to comfort me? Was Carmen letting me see a little glimpse of the afterlife? Was God letting me know that everything was exactly as it should be? Maybe this is something we will never know, but in that instant, joyful laughter broke through the tears that woke me. In that moment, I knew Carmen was happy and celebrating a life well lived. I smile every time I remember that image. The scene that played out for me that morning broke up the intense pain and lifted my spirits enough to get me out of bed. So at the very least, I am certain it was a gift from above; a gift that moved me one step closer to acceptance, and learning to live with yet another excruciating loss.

Is grief the price we pay for having loved? Proof that we truly loved? My friend Charlie Dierkop said when talking about the loss of his only son, "I am grateful to have been able to love someone so much, that it still hurts this much". Charlie's words struck me. We would feel no pain, if we didn't deeply love, right? The more we hurt, the more we know we loved. So when Carmen died, so quickly, and that pain hit, I comforted myself by saying, "I am so lucky to have ever loved someone so much, that it hurts this much". I was so lucky to have him, his unconditional love, in my life for so many years. In his final weeks, after many sleepless nights in the hospital, I saw him, at his weakest, at his saddest, and realized how much I truly, deeply loved his soul. In his final days, he was calling out to his mom, terrified, and that's when I realized we might actually lose him. I climbed into his hospital bed and held him through the night, wanting him to not feel alone, or afraid. All night, I thought about how important he was to my life, my soul, my journey. He was my favorite person on the planet. *How would I carry on without him?*

I was tasked with planning his memorial at The Actors Studio. I didn't know how I was going to do justice to this glorious man who touched so many hearts. I was sad and lost, but I knew enough to remain open. My friends stepped forward fast, offering their services, from music to video editing, photo collecting to event planning. Soon all the right people came together with everything we needed to honor his life and spirit. Many say it was the greatest memorial ever seen at The Actors Studio. "Better than Brando's", they said. It was standing room only and not a dry eye in the house. When it was my time to speak, I didn't know what to say, but knew Carmen would want me to lead. "Raise the bar, Eily", he always said, so in that moment, I decided to share how we helped each other survive our challenges and what we were working on together. He stood beside me for years in my battle for the inclusion of performers with disabilities in film and television. When he was diagnosed with cancer, he asked me to carry on. "Eily, if I die, don't let people waste money on flowers and nonsense. Create a fund, and put that money towards your films that include actors with disabilities. Don't stop. Take over the town, Eily. Please take it over". On that day, many accomplished artists pledged to help us with our films, offering their talents and resources. On that day, I was inspired to carry on, not *without him*, but *FOR HIM*. We honored him with a chair in his name, the very last one available at The Actors Studio. Eight weeks later, two short films were made by teams of people with disabilities, supported by Carmen's memorial fund.

The next few months, in spite of the emotional turmoil, I went through the motions. Telling myself... Just get up. Just keep going. Turn on your happy music. Write. Create. Make Carmen proud. Clean your house. Focus on your work. Make your films. "Take over the town, Eily." Go to new places. Do new things. Do what Carmen would have wanted you to do. Shine! Shine! SHINE!! He wanted you to shine. I asked for signs, and I got them. Often. I even went on a trip by myself to Maui, a place that heals my soul. I cried a lot, processed a lot, and talked to him constantly. I felt he was sending good people and many reminders that he was near.

My strength was slowly returning when I received the call from my younger brother, Joe. His wife Alana was fighting metastatic cancer and they needed me now. We found out it had spread to her brain and spine the same week we found out Carmen had cancer in his brain, so I had been going back and forth across the country trying to help them both survive. Now it was time to go through with Alana what I had just been through with Carmen. It took all my strength to show up with a smile. But I had to. I had to bring love and comfort to Alana, and strength to Joe, no matter how devastated I was feeling inside. I was reliving every moment of losing Carmen, while helping Alana go through the same thing. The next few weeks were the most brutal I have ever seen. Alana was like a sweet Angel, and it was killing us to see her suffer. When it was all over, I sat looking at her box of ashes, and my broken-hearted brother, and knew there was no way out of this, but *through it*. I tried to give him a few bits of hard-earned wisdom, but mostly just unconditional love. All I could really do was let him know I was with him, and understood. Whatever he was feeling, was fine. Let it out. Let it flow.

When I think back on ALL the losses, I learned a lot about how people can make it easier, or make it worse. You feel immense gratitude for those who are KIND through it, those who are gently supportive, those who just allow you to grieve however you need to. It's amazing how many people will judge you or be pushy, giving you unsolicited advice that basically tells you *not to feel*. Not to acknowledge your loss, your pain, *the huge void* left in your heart, and in your life. Those who need you to "get over it" so you can get back to serving *their* life. Those people can do a lot of harm. *Step back from them and trust yourself.* I can tell you from losing my mom nearly 30 years ago, and my dad a few years later, you NEVER get over it. Not if you truly loved. You do, however, learn to live with it.

Slowly, the good memories start to show up. The ones that make you laugh and smile. It is then that we begin to realize just how lucky we were to ever have them in our lives. It is then that we hopefully understand that they will never be gone. They are a huge part of the fabric that is us: *WHO WE ARE.* So rather than let the pain, or other people's expectations, close us off, we have to work hard to remain open. If we can hold on to our capacity to love, we will *add* to the beauty that came before. The next step, the next chapter of our lives, the next adventure is coming. Maybe our loved one will send us our next Angel, but we have to remain grounded and open to all possibilities. Each person we have loved and lost is a part of our foundation, and they will remain a huge part of who we are, but *our* story is not over. There are still many bricks to add to our foundation, our story, our lifetime impact. Each brick that came before was perfect in its own way, and the new bricks will be different, but also perfect, in some way, all adding to the glorious experience of our lives. Our souls were brought together for a reason. We didn't love them because they were perfect. We loved them in spite of their imperfections. And we will again. *Just. Keep. Moving.*

In spite of all the losses, I managed to accomplish quite a lot, mostly because I never stopped trying. All of that pain went into my work. I showed up and did my best, no matter how much I was struggling. Often, no one even knew what was really going on. If there was an opportunity, I said yes, and just kept showing up, even when I didn't know how I was going to do it. Once when trying to wrap my head around an enormous personal loss, Carmen said, "Eily, the way you feel right now, like you've got nothing left to lose, is perfect for the character you are writing in your screenplay. Hang up the phone and write for her *now*." He was right. This is the richness of life and there is a purpose for all of it.

Watch for the signs, the coincidences. I've seen enough to know, *it is bigger than us*. For example, I was struggling to finish this chapter on grief, but when I finally found the courage to bare my soul, I looked at the date. It was my Mother's birthday. Of course. Another sign that I'm exactly where I am supposed to be, doing exactly what I am supposed to be doing.

I believe they are with us, *guiding us every step of the way.*

Bojan Kratofil

Bojan is a full-time book designer/formatter that has worked on over 1,000 books. He is working one to one with award winning authors and publishers to make sure their books are print ready. Many of the books Bojan formatted have reached international bestseller status.

Bojan loves making books come to life.

Connect with Bojan:
https://www.expertformatting.com/
https://twitter.com/FormattingBooks

Chapter 4

Losing My Best Friends

By *Bojan Kratofil*

When I was little, I had a dog name Bubi. I am not exactly sure what breed he was, or I should say that we don't have an English name for this breed. The closest name would be *Small Međimurje Dog (Međi)*. To explain it better, he was a dog who specialized in catching rats. Even though this breed is really small, it's something they are very good at.

Anyway, this story is not about what breed he was, it is about our friendship.

We adopted him when he was really little. He was a really playful puppy. I played with him every day, in the house, outside, in the corn field, wherever I could. He loved to run around the house all the time. I remember him running ten laps of the house without stopping and chasing mice for hours on end. I was tired just watching him.

His favorite food was shell-shaped macaroni with meat. He loved it so much that he could eat a large amount of it in just a few seconds. Also, he loved raspberries. All the raspberries he could get or steal from our neighbor. We even planted a raspberry bush just for him. That's how much he meant to us.

We lived in the countryside, and there weren't many kids living in that area. I rarely went to town, so I didn't have many friends when I was little, just neighbors, so Bubi was my best friend.

One day I went to give him breakfast. Everything was fine and he was really happy (like always) when he saw me. He was happy to see food, but I like to think he was happier to see me!

Then, like every day, he took off to play in the garden. When he came back, I noticed that something wasn't right. He was really tired, but not tired in a good way, after a long day playing. He just didn't look happy. I could see it in his eyes. He looked sad and in pain. My heart felt like it was being torn in half as I never seen him that way. He was always happy and playful, but now all that changed. I didn't know how to help him and make him happy again.

We called the vet right away and described the symptoms over the phone. The vet arrived not long after and checked him out. He told us that Bubi had been poisoned and there was nothing we could do help him.

I was crushed. I didn't know what to do. I saw that he was in a lot of pain, but I just couldn't believe that someone could poison my dog. He had never harmed anyone. He didn't deserve to die.

I couldn't deal with how I felt, and I couldn't watch him suffer, so I took my bike and rode away from home. I kept riding my bike until my legs burned with pain. I cried until I couldn't see through my tears. I couldn't be with him during his last few moments of life because it hurt so much.

When I arrived back home, he was gone. My best friend was gone, and I would never see him again. I was devastated. He didn't deserve to go that way.

It was the first time I had lost a best friend, and I will never forget him.

Žuća

I didn't have another pet for a long time after Bubi died. I couldn't risk loving another animal so much and then have to deal with loss all over again.

It was hard to get over Bubi's death. Every time I saw his doghouse or collar, I cried. I felt like part of me died when I lost him.

Then one day, something happened. My grandma got a cat. She named her Maca. She was beautiful cat. Her coat was brown, white, yellow, orange, and grey; all the colors a cat could have. She was a really good cat, but she never let anyone pet her, except my grandma. I guess she was one of those cats who only loves one person. You all know how cats can be.

I kept trying to win her over, and after weeks of scratched hands, she finally warmed to me. After a while, she would jump on my lap and wait for me to pet her. All those scratches paid off. Even though she was my grandma's cat, we became close and she began to fill the hole in my heart left by Bubi.

***

A few years later, Maca gave birth to five beautiful kittens. One looked like her, one was black, two were grey and one was marmalade.

At the time, we didn't know she was pregnant. I remember one evening Maca went up to the attic and when she came down the next morning, she was much skinnier.

Out of curiosity, I went up to the attic, and I when got up there I found two little black kittens.

I didn't want to disturb them, so I went to see them again a few days later. That's when I saw there were five kittens! I told my mom and she said we'd have to find new homes for some of them, as we couldn't possibly keep them all.

However, as we watched them playing every day and bonded with them, she changed her mind and couldn't bear to see them go to new homes. We had a big back yard so there was room for them all.

We called them Crni (Blackie), Mrvica (Crumb), Mini Maca (because she looked like Maca), Veli (Big one), and Žuća (Yellow one).

As we now had six cats in total, we didn't keep them in the house at night. Each night, my mom would lead them to the barn, and, each morning we would let them out to eat and play.

And, from the moment I saw Žuća, I knew he would be "my cat". He ate, slept and played with me. We were together constantly, and I definitely spoiled him. He was so spoiled that he even slept on my lap while I would eat dinner at the table.

One day, my mom went out to get milk from the goats. For some reason, *Žuća* decided to go with her. Later we realized how smart he was and why he went. He knew that goats were milked, so he would go with my mom, hoping to get some milk for himself. Eventually, my mom would bring a bowl for him so he could have some every day.

A few years later, I started at a high school that was a few kilometers away. Each morning, when I would get ready for school, Žuća wanted to come with me. My mom would have to come after me and bring him home. Eventually, she would have to hold him to stop him from following me.

In the evening he would be waiting for me when I got home from school. Every day he came a little further up the road until he was halfway between my school and our house. He was more like a dog than a cat in a lot of ways.

Unfortunately, we eventually lost all the cats. Maca died when she was sixteen. Crni and Veli went missing. Eli actually came back three months later, but, unfortunately, a few months later, he went missing again and he never came back.

On the other hand, Žuća was always there. He never went missing or became ill. He was with me. Always waiting for me on my walk home from school.

***

One day when I went to school, something really terrible happened. I fed and played with him as I did every morning.

When I walked home from school that evening, Žuća wasn't there to meet me. I felt like something was very wrong, so I ran the rest of the way home.

When I got back, I noticed that my mom looked sad. And when I looked around, I couldn't see Žuća anywhere. Then my mom told me what happened. A car had hit him. He was gone.

I couldn't believe it. My heart was crushed again. It was like Bubi all over again and I just couldn't deal with the pain. I had lost another friend.

I was so sad that I couldn't go to school, and when I did go to school, I wasn't really present. I was overcome with sadness.

I remember coming home and looking for him, hoping to see him running towards me. But, sadly, that didn't happen. He was gone.

Even now, after many years passed, I still look at the place where he waited for me. I still have all his toys and I will always keep them to remind me how happy I was when I had him.

***

After Bubi and Žuća, I promised myself that I would never have a pet again. And I kept that promise for over ten years.

I have of course broken that promise, and now I have two beautiful dogs Kika and Max, who are mom and son.

When I think about everything that happened, I am reminded of the movie, *A Dog's Journey*. I lost Bubi a long time ago and he came back in the form of Žuća, and years later, he came back in a form of Kika and Max.

In a way, Bubi was always here with me.

It is very hard when you lose your pet, someone who was with you all the time, who was your best friend in all the good and bad times. But, sometimes, faith brings them back to you and all that void in your heart is filled again. When you experience loss, keep your heart open to new experiences. They will help you to heal.

Bernadette Bingham

The second oldest of 14 children, Bernadette grew up on a farm near Saginaw Michigan in the USA. The mother of two daughters and 7 amazing grandchildren, Bernadette recently lost her husband and soulmate to a sudden, tragic death after almost 46 years of marriage.

Retired as the Vice President of the Saginaw County Chamber of Commerce, Bernadette is currently owner of "21st Century SOLUTIONS" which organizes and facilitates membership and sponsorship campaigns for non profit organizations.

Bernadette was a contributing author to the best -selling collaborative book - The Missing Piece in Forgiveness. She enjoys organizing and facilitating women's growth and inner healing groups and spiritually mentoring women.

You can be reach Bernadette at
Email:babingham@outlook.com
Phone:. 989 245 6977

Chapter 5

My Marc

By *Bernadette Bingham*

Current Day:
August 3, 2019 - 9 months

My Darling, Precious Marc,
It's been 9 months since we sat in the living room and talked and laughed out loud. 9 months since you told me you love me. 9 months since you kissed me and held me.

47 years side by side with you and just like that you're gone. Sometimes it feels like forever. More often it feels like yesterday.

I miss you so much. I miss the talking and laughing and hugging and loving with you. I miss traveling with you and going out to lunch or shows, or just watching TV with you.

I miss having you in our big king size bed every night or seeing you doze in your chair. I miss the quirky half grin when you teased me and your intense blue eyes that looked right into my soul when we conversed. I miss your voice and your laughter. Oh, how I miss your voice and laughter!!!

I miss everything about you. I miss **YOU!**

My Marc, you and I had a conversation just days before your death on how blessed we were to have the relationship we had. That it was the kind of coupleness that so many seek, and we were gifted with that special gift of deep passion and respect, of contentment, acceptance, and love of each other. You and I always thanked God for His Grace in our marriage.

We talked about the Marriage Encounter we experienced some 40+ years ago that started us on the journey of allowing God to be a full Partner in our marriage and for all the people who have influenced us over the years. And we expressed gratefulness that God gave us the willingness to do the hard work that is necessary for any marriage to work. We learned not to take our relationship with each other for granted. We knew we were blessed. I'm so grateful for that conversation.

I would never have dreamed, 47 years ago, that you and I would be so happy and complete each other so well. Remember the night we met on the blind date? You barely talked all night but you were such a gentleman, holding doors, making sure I had everything I needed and taking care with me as we walked on the icy surfaces outdoors. I was impressed.

We married within a year and had two beautiful daughters and now 7 amazing grandchildren who each are the center of our hearts. We've had our ups and downs, but God led us to grow in love for each other and for Him.

Marc, you helped many married couples have stronger relationships as we ministered through Marriage Encounter, Marriage Enrichments and personal mentoring. For over 47 years you sponsored many members of Alcoholics Anonymous. You became an 'adopted' father and papa to many. You opened up our home to those that did not have food or home or family. You gave people money with no expectation of return. You worked with troubled youth and many of them choose to have healthier more productive lives just because you shared yourself and your faith with them. You worked with traumatized Viet Nam Veterans, sometimes listening, sometimes sharing, and sometimes just holding them while they wept. You touched so many people in so many different ways.

You invested yourself in being there for others and helping them heal and grow. You loved without condition. I am so proud to be your wife.

Day 1
November 3, 2018:

The hospital called tonight and said I needed to come because you'd been in a serious automobile accident. When I heard about the accident I didn't know what to pray for. I knew you didn't want to have spine or head injuries or a life of being crippled or in pain. I gave you to God and asked God to do whatever was best for you. When I arrived there, they told me you had passed away.

It's so surreal. I'm stunned and in shock.

When the doctor told me you had passed away, I accepted that was God's answer to my prayer and I was, and am, grateful to God for the 47 years of love we shared with each other. The police said you were driving home from the store and ran a stop sign. You flipped and ended up in a big water filled ditch. They believe you drowned in the ditch as you were non response when they arrived.

Oh, Marc. They said you T-boned another vehicle and a 14-year old girl was killed at the scene. Her father was critically injured. I was overwhelmed with horror and grief for her family and loved ones. I was and am deeply grateful that you died without being aware of her death. I know it would have been the most difficult thing you would have ever experienced if you knew you had contributed to her death. You were the best driver I've ever known. It makes no sense at all that you ran a stop sign. It is so agonizing for all of us to know this. I have so much grief and profound sadness for the child's family. Sometimes I feel like I can't breathe. I can't even begin to understand their loss and pain. I can only pray for them and trust that God is with them as He is with me.

"Dear God, thank you for taking Marc Home with You. Please give us Your strength. We need You."

Day 6
November 8, 2018

Today was visitation at the funeral home. Several hundred came to pay their respects. You are so respected and loved. I'm overwhelmed at the caring of so many. The Chief of Police phoned me this morning and told me the autopsy showed you had a massive heart attack that killed you before you even hit the water. The heart attack is what they believe caused the accident and I was told there was nothing you could have done to prevent it.

Many people ask me if I am relieved by the autopsy results. I am deeply grateful and relieved that you weren't negligent or careless. It was awful for us to live with that idea these past few days. But the Medical Examiner ruling in no way negates the fact that another person lost her life, another family will forever grieve, because your paths crossed in the worst possible way.

Not your "fault", not your choice, but reality, nevertheless. One mere second either way and you would still have died from the heart attack, but it would be only our family grieving.

It's seems so unfair, so wrong. I can't understand why this had to happen to such a gifted, beautiful child. I'm struggling not to feel guilty or be angry. I will never forget nor cease to feel a deep level of the pain for this family and their loss. I'm sure the cause of death – the cause of the accident – is a footnote to them. The horrible reality is they lost their child And I don't understand why you, My Marc, are part of this horrific tragedy. You've made such a life changing, positive difference in so many lives. I'm so sorry and so confused that this is the way you left us.

"Dear Lord, please be with both of our families today and comfort us with your love and serenity. We need You so much."

Two Weeks
November 14, 2018

My Marc, two weeks ago you sat in your chair and pulled me onto your lap just to hold me and hug me. Tonight, I curled up in your chair with your remains and hugged you and wept for your absence in this world while I praised God for the gift you were to me and so many. It seems impossible that so much can change so drastically, so permanently in such a short period of time.

I wish I had teased you more, hugged you more and expressed my appreciation and love more to you that day. I wish I had gone with you. You would still be gone but you wouldn't have died alone. Maybe we would have stopped to see the kids or gotten a bite to eat. Maybe it would have changed our timetable and maybe the child could have been spared.

"Coulda, woulda, shoulda". These are among the most unproductive words in our language. The day was what it was. Nothing can change that. In this life I will never understand what happened that day. My God does not preordain, He does not manipulate, He did not "make" this happen, and I totally don't believe it was His will. It just is. I could make myself crazy trying to figure out an answer where there is no answer.

I am clinging to the words from Romans 8:26 for my sake and the sake of all affected by the accident: *"We know that God makes all things work together for the good of those who love Him....."*
In the midst of the pain of overwhelming sadness and loss I am also feeling deeply humbled and grateful because I know God is with me.

"Thank You, Lord, for Your Promise. Just thank you."

4 Months
March 10, 2019

Time often stands still for me. I still don't comprehend in my heart that you are forever gone from this world. It still feels like you'll be home shortly. It feels like you left minutes ago to go to the store. It feels like it happened yesterday. I have little concept of time.

So often, everything is still so surreal and I'm still in shock mode. 4 months ago, I didn't know the world existed that I am now immersed in every single day. I never knew I could feel such pain as the loss I feel since you've left this earth. I still find it beyond comprehension that you're gone. That you left so suddenly, in such an unspeakable, confusing way. You were here then, in a split second, poof, you were just gone.

Every day I am grateful for the amazing, unconditional love you always had (and I know still have) for me. The unconditional acceptance of just who I am, the total package that is me. You were never shy about telling me how much you loved me and how much you valued me. Your words of love are etched in my memory and my heart and I am so, so grateful that God chose to put you and I together and that He blessed us with His hope and faith and His unconditional love.

"My Lord, You have opened my eyes and my heart this year to so many people who love me and are there for me. I am humbled and so profoundly grateful. Thank You."

7 months
June 2, 2019

The past couple of months have been so difficult, so sad, so lonely, so depressing. I feel so empty. I can't think, can't feel, I can't make decisions. So many who have walked this journey before me have said their grief is measured in years, not days, weeks or months. My therapist concurs.

I hate this. I HATE this whole thing. I never knew anything could be so difficult, so painful, and so incredibly lonely. Marc, I miss you so much. I miss your jokes, your laughter, your wisdom, your tenderness, your loving presence.

I know so many ladies who have lost their husbands in recent years. And I had no clue what they were going through. Once the funeral was over, I guess I figured that the worst was over. How naïve I was. Yet I look around and see so many who have the same, too often even a more painful and tragic loss than I.

I'm so humbled by the strength, courage and faith of so many who have reached out to me in the midst of their own pain.
"I trust You, Lord, totally. Thank you."

9 months
Current Day (continued)
August 3, 2019

I've grown to be at peace with you being gone, my Marc. I know you are with Jesus and our Father, in a place of perfect love and joy. It gives me great joy to know you have no more pain, no more sorrow, no more PTSD and the nightmares of war that come with it. You are surrounded by God's Glory and you are at peace. I am in awe.

It's a whole new thing to plug into a totally spiritual relationship with you, Marc. You have spoken to my heart and let me know you love me more now than you ever did with the perfect love God fills you with every single day. I know you are watching out for me, that you are proud of me and that you are praying for me. I know someday we will be with each other again, in a very different way than we were here on earth.

My anger about the precious little girl's death is gone. A profound sadness fills my heart for her family, and I have an assurance that God is with them as He is with me. I trust He has a plan for them as He does for me and I am grateful for God's faithfulness.

My life and my future are so different since you left, Marc. I'm different. I'm calmer. I don't sweat the small stuff as much. It's easier to accept the things I can't change. I don't worry as much. I'm more grateful. God is more real to me.

I don't fear death. I know Heaven is real. I believe death is a beautiful and special gift. God's Word says: "*Well done My good and faithful servant.*" and "*Eye has not seen nor ear heard what God has prepared for us*". What an amazing promise.

Some days I struggle with loneliness, depression, and fear. I weep often, at the strangest times. I hurt. I miss you so much, My Marc. When I focus on my loss, my pain is agonizing. But in the middle of that storm of pain and loss, when I choose to focus on God, I have a strong sense of His serenity and a deep gratitude for how blessed my life has been, is and will continue to be if I continue to keep my eyes on God and trust Him.

God is teaching me so much right now on what I call my Journey. My trust that God has a Plan for me and that He'll take care of me is stronger than ever. This is a gift I don't take for granted. It humbles me. It carries me. It heals me. I am grateful. I love you, My Marc, today and forever. Thank you for always loving me so well.

"Dear Lord, My God,
You are teaching me so much right now.

You are teaching me about your unconditional love through the love Marc showed and continues to have for me every day. I am so darned grateful for the life journey You have blessed me with. Thank You for Your Faithfulness to Marc and to me. I praise You, Lord, just because You are You.

You are showing me I have often been unaware of the pain experienced by others who have lost loved ones. Lord, You have opened my eyes and my heart to so many who are suffering so much pain and loss in their lives. I ask You to be with them in their grief. Gift them with the assurance that You are truly with them and that You are totally trustworthy in all things. Please bless them with Your serenity and may they know Your hope and unconditional, forever love.

You are teaching me that serenity, gratitude, and love are found by keeping my eyes on You instead of my own pain.

Please be with both families from Marc's accident and give us all Your peace and deepen our faith in You.

Lord, I love You.

In Jesus Name, thank You. Amen"

Lynda Cheldelin Fell

Lynda Cheldelin Fell is co-founder of the International Grief Institute and international bestselling author of over 30 books including the award-winning Grief Diaries series. She is a certified critical incident stress management educator dedicated to supporting community resilience through best practice strategies. Lynda has earned five national literary awards and five national advocacy award nominations for her work.

Learn more at:

www.LyndaFell.com

www.GriefDiaries.com/
www.internationalgriefinstitute.com

Email: lynda@lyndafell.com
facebook.com/lynda.cheldelin.fell

Chapter 6

The Playbook of Hope

By *Lynda Cheldelin Fell*

One night in 2007, I had a vivid dream. I was the front passenger in a car and my teen daughter Aly was sitting behind the driver. Suddenly, the car missed a curve in the road and sailed into a lake. The driver and I escaped the sinking car, but Aly did not. As I bobbed to the surface, I dove again and again in the murky water searching desperately for my daughter. But I failed to find her. She was gone. My beloved daughter was gone, leaving nothing but an open book floating on the water where she disappeared.

Two years later, on August 5, 2009, that horrible nightmare became reality when Aly died as a backseat passenger in a car accident. Returning home from a swim meet, the car carrying Aly was T-boned by a father coming home from work. My beautiful fifteen-year-old daughter took the brunt of the impact and died instantly. She was the only fatality.

Just when I thought life couldn't get any worse, it did. My dear sweet hubby buried his grief in the sand. He escaped into eighty-hour workweeks, more wine, more food, and less talking. His blood pressure shot up, his cholesterol went off the chart, and the perfect storm arrived on June 4, 2012. Suddenly, he began drooling and couldn't speak. My 46-year-old soulmate was having a major stroke.

My husband survived the stroke but couldn't speak, read, or write, and his right side was paralyzed. Still reeling from the loss of our daughter, I found myself again thrust into a fog of grief so thick I couldn't see through the storm. Adrenaline and autopilot resumed their familiar place at the helm.

Facing what felt like a lifetime of grief, I didn't think I could endure the agony, and many days I didn't want to. How could I learn to live with my child in my heart instead of my arms? Would my husband ever be the same? I didn't know what the future held, and I didn't want to find out.

My playbook began in that fog of anguish, the first chapter blank except for a firestorm of indescribable pain. Every breath was pure agony

The next few chapters were filled with wailing and the gnashing of teeth. Desperate for relief, I then embarked on a fraught search for comfort, a respite from the agony.

The end of my playbook remains unwritten but the chapters up to this point have taught me many important lessons, chief among them is that the human heart can hold joy the same time as sorrow.

It's hard to believe hope and happiness are possible when we can't see past the pain. But as the rawness softens and our coping skills strengthen, loss can become a catalyst for change—and a gateway to collateral blessings.

But when the anguish and sadness are so profound, how do we find the energy and strength to face the grief and process our loss? How do we survive?

The answer is simple: We survive by facing each moment one at a time, then using very small steps to get through them.

On the following pages are the baby steps I took to put hell in my rear-view mirror. Each step took great effort at first coupled with lots of patience, but like any dedicated routine it got easier with time. And the reward of restoring happiness to my life was worth every step.

Baby Step #1: Get out of bed

In the early days of profound grief, exhaustion sets in easily prompting many to give up before the day has even begun. After all, what difference does it make whether we grieve in bed or grieve in the kitchen? At least in bed, we can pull the covers over our head in an attempt to shut out reality, right?

As it is with every substantial challenge, we always have a choice. And for those experiencing profound grief, that first choice is whether to get out of bed. Or not.

Getting out of bed itself is symbolic for hope – hope of survival, hope that the pain will eventually lessen, hope that we might figure out how to put one foot in front of the other. It also avails us to the support we desperately need.

Even if you go about your day in just pyjamas holding a big box of tissue, you've taken the first step every morning to greet your day, however painful it may be.

Yes, one must dig deep within to find the strength to face the fresh devastation that each morning brings. Yet, with time, choosing to get out of bed offers us so many more possibilities. Staying in bed offers us nothing but delay in our effort to reassemble the pieces of our life.

Baby Step #2: TLC

During intense grief, it can be helpful to consider yourself in the intensive care unit of Grief United Hospital and treat accordingly. If your best friend were in the ICU, how would you treat him or her? With kindness, compassion, and love. Now make yourself your own best friend.

Give yourself a little tender loving care using the Rule of 5. Simply put, treat your five senses to something that looks, feels, smells, tastes, and sounds good. Using the Rule of 5 below, find ways to offer yourself some form of sensorial pleasure every day. With practice, the awareness of delight eventually becomes effortless, and is an important step toward restoring happiness.

THE RULE OF 5:

- 5 things you can see
- 4 things you can touch
- 3 things you can hear
- 2 things you can smell
- 1 thing you can taste

If wearing fuzzy blue socks offers a smidgen of comfort, then wear them unabashedly. If whipped cream on your cocoa offers a morsel of pleasure, then indulge unapologetically.

Profound grief can appear to rob our world of all beauty. Yet the truth is, and despite our suffering, beauty continues to surround us. The birds continue to sing, flowers continue to bloom, the surf continues to ebb and flow. Soothing your five senses by doing things that evokes sensorial joy can help you destress and relax, and serve as important reminders that not all pleasure is lost.

SUGGESTIONS:

- Shower or bathe with a lovely, scented soap (scent)
- Soak in a warm tub with Epsom salts or bath oil (touch)
- Wear a pair of extra soft socks (touch)
- Light a fragrant candle (scent)
- Listen to relaxing music (sound)
- Apply a rich lotion to your skin before bed (touch, scent)
- Indulge in a few bites of your favorite treat (taste)
- Enjoy a mug of your favorite soothing herbal tea (taste)
- Add whipped cream to a steaming mug of cocoa (taste)
- Watch a comedy (sight, sound)
- Wrap yourself in a soft scarf (touch)
- Listen to the birds sing (sound)
- Watch a sunset (sight)

- Walk through a flower garden (sight, scent)

Reconnecting with our surroundings helps us to reintegrate back into our environment, so find ways to offer yourself tender loving care every day. With practice, the awareness of delight eventually becomes effortless, and is an important step toward regaining joy.

Baby Step #3: Give joy

Winston Churchill once said, "We make a living by what we get. We make a life by what we give." In other

words, helping others helps our own heart to heal.

Giving is good for the giver in that it induces a natural high. It also evokes internal gratitude which helps to heal our heart. Additional bonuses are the multiple health benefits including lower blood pressure, increased self-esteem, less depression, lower stress, and greater happiness.

Here are some easy ways to engage in giving:

- Volunteer in the community
- Donate to a charity
- Feed the homeless in a soup kitchen
- Random acts of kindness
- Leave balloons in a park for children to find
- Distribute Blessing Bags to the homeless
- Hold the door open for someone behind you
- Smile at a stranger
- Send an anonymous care package to someone in need

Additional bonuses are the multiple and proven health benefits of giving less stress, lower blood pressure, improved sleep, increased self-esteem, and greater happiness. Truly, she who heals others heals herself.

Baby Step #4: Protect your health

After our daughter's accident I soon found myself fighting an assortment of viruses including head colds, stomach flus, sore throats and more, compounding my already frazzled emotions. It was then that I realized how far reaching the effects of grief has, that it truly touches every part of our life including our physical health.

Studies show that profound grief throws our body into "flight or fight" syndrome for months and months. This prolonged physiological response can often cause physical unbalance that leads to adrenal fatigue. This, in turn, results in compromised immunity and illnesses. Thus, it becomes critical to guard our physical health.

Resist the urge to seek refuge in damaging substances such as alcohol or illicit drugs. Instead, nourish your body by way of healthful eating, small amounts of light exercise such as walking with a friend, and doing your best to practice good sleep and hygiene. A stronger physical health can help anchor us in times of emotional upheaval.

Baby Step #5: Find an Outlet

In the early part of the journey, everything is painful. What used to be routine activities, such as moving about, breathing, and eating, are all now exceedingly excruciating.

Finding something to distract you from the pain, occupy your mind, and soothe your senses can be tricky, but possible.

Three months after our daughter's accident, my dear husband and I sought refuge in a quaint little town on a nearby island. While browsing through the boutiques with a heavy heart, I stopped to admire a basket of highly fragrant soaps. On a whim, I decided to teach myself how to make soap and soon discovered that the soothing action of stirring a pot of fragrant ingredients proved to be very therapeutic. Thus, making Tear Soap became my vent for many months.

SUGGESTIONS:

• Learn to mold chocolate or make soap

• Learn to bead, knit, crochet, or quilt

• Volunteer in the community

• Learn a new sport such as golf or kayaking

• Create a garden in a forgotten part of the yard

• Join Pinterest or a book club

• Doodle, draw, or mold clay

• Scrapbook

Finding a creative outlet for sorrow can lead to some lovely treasures. Learning to bead can result in beautiful gifts of jewelry. Learning to mold chocolate can be very soothing and delicious. Digging into an ignored corner of weeds can result in a beautiful memorial garden.

Most important, performing a peaceful repetitive act can soothe your physical senses and calm your mood, and can result in a new craft or a few treasured gifts made from the heart of hearts.

Where am I today?

Today I'm often asked how I manage my grief so well. Some assume that because I found peace and joy, I'm avoiding my grief. Others believe that because I work in the bereavement field, I'm wallowing in self-pity.

Well, which is it?

Neither.

I miss my child with every breath I take. Just like you, I will always have my moments and triggers: the painful holidays, birthdays, death anniversaries, a song or smell that evokes an unexpected memory. But I have also found purpose, beauty and joy again.

It takes hard work and determination to overcome profound grief, and it also takes the ability to let go and succumb to the journey. Do not be afraid of the tears, sorrow, and heartbreak; after all, they are a natural human reaction. Most important, they're imperative to healing.

There is a vast assortment of tools to help you along the journey, each created by someone who walked in your shoes and understands the heartache. Collect a toolbox of whatever tools feel best. Although many wonderful resources are available, what brings comfort to one might irritate the next. If one tool doesn't work, find another.

The five baby steps above are just that—baby steps. As small as they are, they helped me tremendously.

While they don't erase or invalidate the pain in your heart, the truth is that if you treat yourself kindly, allow yourself small measures of comfort, and find a healthy outlet for your grief, you'll feel better. And if you feel better, you'll cope better.

Ten years ago, I didn't want to live. But what I didn't know then that I know now is that life's second act was worth fighting for. Hope and happiness are possible after loss. I promise. The key is to fight for it. Begin here and now.

Start with my baby steps above and keep going. Baby steps are better than no steps. And remember that there's a bright future at every turn, even if you miss one.

Michelle Clayton

Michelle Clayton is a business owner, and a single mother to 3 growing boys, Michelle's priority in anything she does is always keeping her family first.

Due to the sad passing of her mum 13 years ago, Michelle is determined to live life at the fullest in everything she does.

Email: michellewhittington84@yahoo.com

Chapter 7

Very Little Time

By Michelle Clayton

When Kate invited me to write a chapter for this book I didn't realize until I started to write it how much grief stays with you and how much you think you have healed, yet, you haven't. The grief is still lurking under a thin layer beneath your emotions. When I started writing about the experience of losing my mum to cancer them emotions rose to the surface and it felt like I was reliving the experience all over again.

I remember it like it was yesterday, it was a Friday evening and I had just received a phone call from my mum to ask me if I could take her to see the doctor because she mentioned she was still not feeling very well. Even though I was 7 months pregnant and not feeling 100% brilliant myself, I still got up to place on my shoes, grabbed my car keys and headed for the door.

I remember feeling worried as I left the house, I knew I didn't want to leave anything to chance with it only being 2 years prior that she was treated for breast cancer and was placed on chemotherapy. Even though she had been in remission for 2 years, there was always the niggling feeling at the back of my mind that it could come back. My pregnancy, however, was slowing me down. I was 8 weeks away from giving birth to my first baby and I felt terrible with this being quite a challenging pregnancy it had zapped all my energy. I just wanted to give birth, feel better and have my energy back so that everything did not feel like I had to force myself to do it.

I slowly placed myself into the car and went to pick up mum from her apartment to take her to the doctor's surgery. While we were sitting in the doctor's surgery, I could read the worry and stress on her face and she was extremely worried that the cancer had come back and sat nervously waiting to see what the doctor had to say. After listening to my mum describe her symptoms the doctor advised her to go to the hospital straight away for tests and so he called the hospital to have her admitted. Even though we knew this was the best thing to do it never really stops the panic in your mind when a doctor admits your mum straight to the hospital. However, amid the panic, we tried to stay as positive as possible and knew the tests would give us the answers we need, and that mum would be in the best possible place if anything was wrong.

I took her back to her apartment to help her pack her hospital bag and after we gathered her things, we stopped by my apartment to pick up a few things and inform other family members that mum was going to be admitted to hospital for further tests. As she sat there on my sofa drinking a glass of milk waiting for me while I rushed around like a headless chicken, I wish I had known now what I didn't know at that moment in time. I wish I had known that this would be the last time she would ever sit on my sofa, forever. Only, we never truly know what is around the corner until it happens.

When we reached the hospital, my mum was taken straight onto the hospital ward and shown to her bed where she was told to make herself comfortable and the doctor would be with her as soon as possible. Whilst we sat on the bed waiting for the doctor, we both held my tummy giving love to the unborn child inside of me. Mum could feel the baby kicking her hand and I spoke softly through a smile saying "Mum, if you wake him, he will have me up half the night kicking me and my back hurts already." Mum apologized and said she couldn't help the excitement of her first grandchild's birth, and all the things she has planned for when he arrived. Mum had her heart set on taking my baby off my hands every Thursday to help me with the feeding and changing while I could rest and recover after birth. The excitement in her voice of describing all of this was reassuring that she had so much to live for and so much more joy to experience.

Two days into mum's hospital stay I received the terrible news that the cancer had come back, I felt like the floor had just opened and swallowed me whole. I couldn't quite take in what I was hearing when we were told cancer had spread from behind her breast scare tissue to her stomach and liver.

The doctors immediately placed her on to a high dose of chemotherapy in hope to save her life and she was provided painkillers for the pain. Witnessing my mum hooked up to all these different machines to help fight this horrible disease was devastating and it took me back to when my nana passed away 17 years before. The memories of receiving that sad news were now resurfacing, it was like this was history repeating itself and I didn't know how to cope with all these emotions at once.

The chemotherapy and painkillers had such an effect on mum that she seemed to have completely zoned out and stopped communicating, it was like she was on a completely different planet. I didn't like this one bit and without the ability to communicate with my mom, my best friend, my rock I suddenly felt so lonely and confused about what was happening?

The doctor took us into a side room to speak to us and there he broke the devastating news, that nothing else could be done and that the cancer had spread too much throughout mum's body to control it. The only thing the hospital could do now was to make her comfortable and they advise me that she had only 2 months to live, maximum. I couldn't breathe, and I couldn't take in what was being said I started to panic and almost collapsed on the floor crying out that she has to survive because she has her first grandchild on the way, plus, we've been through so much in the last 10 years which we managed to survive so how could she leave us now? So many questions? So much confusion and so much pain ripped through me I felt like my heart had just been torn out my chest.

The 2 months that the doctor predicted mum had left to live was only 2 days, the hospital rang me the following morning to advise all the family to come in and say our last goodbyes. We all gathered at mum's hospital bed side at 1:10 am as she started to struggle with her breathing. Once Allan arrived at 1:18am mum took her last breath and passed away. We know she would have held on until Allan arrived before she knew it was time to let go.

It has now been 13 years since my mum grew her angel wings and left us behind and life has been far from easy. It's hard to deal with not having her there when I need her the most, it's even more difficult having to explain to my 3 boys why their grandmother isn't here and why she was taken away too soon. I find myself struggling sometimes to place into words for these 3 young children to understand how amazing, loving and caring she was.

I constantly tell the memories I have had of when I was a child with her and I just say to them if I am half the mum that she was then I'll be doing an ok job, which sometimes I wish there was a way that she could tell me how I was doing and confirm I am doing it right.

Nothing in this world can ever prepare you for the loss of a loved one. You can get lost in this pretence that it will never happen to you which leads to you taking life for granted. When I lost my mum, I felt so alone and even though I was surrounded by other family members, I know that each one of us was locked inside our grief and dealing with it in our way. Personally, for me, I felt I had done something wrong and that I was being punished for something, which left me so angry that she had to leave me so soon. I was so angry with Cancer, the fact it caused her so much pain, hair loss and robbed her of ever seeing her grandchildren.

People say that time is a great healer, and that it gets easier to deal with your grief. To be honest, I think we busy ourselves to not truly face the fact that it never gets easier, grief just becomes a part of your everyday life. You just need to live the best life you want to live while you can because life can be so short. Mum was only 44 years young when she passed-away, and her life had only just begun.

To this day I still miss her so much, and sometimes wish I could just pick up the phone and call her and tell her the achievements my children have made that week at school. But, I can't do that and the only way I can keep her memory alive is by taking the boys to the cemetery so they can place flowers on her grave, place many photos of her around the house and continue to tell stories from my memory. This way I still feel that she is a part of their lives even though they never got to meet her, and I know they would have loved her as much as I did, and still do.

Vicki Mona Savoie

Dedicated entrepreneur, advocate and author, Vicki Mona Savoie has never been one to sit on the sidelines when there's a difference to be made.

Excelling in her career as a corporate office administrator for numerous years, she still found time to support and inspire co-workers as the vice president of a prominent trade union.

As an active board member for select non-profits, she also volunteered at the extended care facility where her aging father was a resident, an eye-opening experience for Vicki Mona which truly underscored the need for more effective information sharing for both seniors and caregivers, and prompted her to write her enlightening *Extended Journey* memoirs.

Championing the needs of rural women in her role as a thriving sales diva on-the-go, Vicki Mona now runs a successful business retailing premier nail care accessories and high fashion jewelry while promoting increased confidence and self-esteem.

Multi-talented yet single-minded, when following her passion, there's no doubt that this dynamic change-maker gets involved!

Chapter 8

A Good Old Boy

By Vicki Mona Savoie

The small envelope was delivered on a beautiful prairie summer day, close to my birthday. Addressed to me, it was surely a card, I thought, but sadly, this fateful envelope contained unexpected news that brought not the anticipated smiles, but, instead, a rush of sudden tears. Decades of memories flooded my mind as I read the invitation.

"My brother is in palliative care. I am reaching out to friends to see if you would care to come and visit him."

Rodney Joseph Pollom had been my first love. The Universe moves people through our lives all the time, but it's incredible how specific memories stay indelibly imprinted in our minds, our hearts, and in our souls. With a pang of overwhelming nostalgia, I recalled my experiences with Rod and how he'd influenced my life from as far back as early childhood.

I was just a curious four-year-old visiting my aunt's rural home with my father when I interrupted their conversation that day, demanding to see the boy on a horse they were discussing. It was the mention of the horse that first caught my attention, far more interesting than any boy. I clearly remember Auntie saying that he rode past her farm every day on his way to work. Why wasn't he in school instead, and did Daddy know that his sister got married? What did I care? I was only interested in seeing the horse and, okay, perhaps this intriguing boy.

Kindly granting my wish, Father hiked me up onto his shoulders so I could see the duo pass by. I had no idea who he was; I didn't care about his sister. At that moment, I only wanted to see that boy and the horse. Alas, the distance made them seem so small. Oh, how I wished we would stay over with Auntie, so I could get a closer look the next morning, but it was not to be.

I now believe this very first introduction to Rod was a significant message. Because I was so young, however, I didn't realize the important place he would hold in my life. Eleven years would pass before I saw that boy again, now a grown man.

My mother, aunt, and I were visiting the farm of a dear family friend I called Uncle Lawrence. That particular morning, we had accompanied the men to the field to help move hay bales. The blistering sun burning the dew off the ground was creating a warm, soft-edged mist that made the whole countryside look like something out of dream, when, materializing through that hot, summer haze, Rod Pollom appeared in my life again, as he walked past us to greet the men.

"Who is that guy?" I asked. *"Oh, that's Rod, uncle Mike's son, home for a visit."* Auntie quipped, as if I should already know. *"He's here on leave from the northern oil rigs where he works."*

Ever the loyal son, Rod had been helping his parents build the family farm from the time he was tall enough to sit on a stool and milk cows. The oldest son of thirteen children, he was a shoulder to lean on and a willing helping hand, not at all shy about dispensing unsolicited advice to his siblings. His deep love of horses had continued to be an integral part of his identity, whether he watched from the side-lines as a dedicated rodeo fan, or competed himself on horseback in the team roping or gymkhana events. Rod was a good old boy, a cowboy at heart.

At the tender age of fifteen, he'd begun an oilfield career that gave him the ability to help his family. Knowledgeable, hardworking and reliable, Rod was now universally loved and respected, a petroleum industry pioneer. Following that compelling trail of black gold, he'd continued to work throughout Alberta's most remote areas, running the first service rigs into Rainbow Lake and Swan Hills before those town sites even existed.

That summer day, Rod wore white Levi jeans, a white western shirt with pearl snap buttons and brown cowboy boots. He looked like he'd just walked off a western movie set ready to attend a dance rather than pitch bales of hay in the heat, but, there he was. While the sun played tricks; I shaded my eyes with my hand, all I could see was Rod's back as he moved through that dreamy haze of light as if walking right into the sun. Rolling up his sleeves, Rod grabbed a pitchfork and started working along with the others. The momentary spell was broken.

I didn't pay much more attention to him as the afternoon wore on, being too preoccupied with the freedom of smoking cigarettes without anyone bugging me. The sun beat down on us as we lifted bale after bale onto the wagons occasionally stopping for a puff and, of course, a sip. By the time the adults finally had enough of the sweltering heat, it was determined that I should ride back to the farm with Rod. Embarrassed protests secretly made to my mother fell on deaf ears. She told me if I wanted a ride back home, he was the guy who had room in his car.

Since I had no choice and clearly, my mother thought is was permissible for me to ride with this stranger, I reluctantly climbed in. The memory is still with me. Sitting as close to the passenger door as possible it was as though I'd glued myself to the red leather. I'm sure he sensed my concern since he broke the silence by offering me a cigarette. Soft-spoken and kind, he asked questions, even acted interested when I told him about school and my family back in the city. I liked him; he listened to me. I was flattered to have the attention of a good-looking, older guy who had a cool car. One thing Rod forgot to ask was my age. Looking back, I was much too young to fall in love, but, as summer wore on, I did.

With his family farm only a short distance away; Rod was a daily visitor to the Pollom Ranch, as we named it, a property owned by his Uncle Lawrence, who was also our family's friend. There was always something to do on the farm, someone to visit or someplace to go. Happily, Rod always invited me to tag along. Those idyllic summer months ended much too soon. Rod went back to the rigs, and I went back to school.

Keeping in touch was quite a challenge before the days of cell towers. At that time the only available communication in the bush was through two-way mobile radiophones or "bag phones". Calls from those phones presented a baffling challenge to master that I could somehow never get right, always forgetting to say "over" to continue the conversation. The first time he called, I hung up on him, thinking the line had gone dead! Rod would regale me with stories of working up north on the oilrigs where his job compelled him to stay for months at a time. The pay was right, though. He intended to follow that black gold money trail wherever it would lead. We muddled through the calls making plans for his next time off during the spring break up.

That next summer was a whirlwind with a twist, Rod being quite intent on ensuring I was better acquainted with his family. He was courting me, of course, but, without the necessary life experience, I was clueless as to his true objectives. What did I know? I was always delivered back to the Pollom Ranch at days end, with one exception. The one night we stayed over with his family, I recall admiring his showmanship as he played the fiddle to resounding applause. When the delightful evening came to an end, I slept in a big bed with Rod's mother. She asked about my life, what I wanted to do when school was complete. I mentioned I was interested in becoming a teacher; not having previously given any career plans much attention. I was soon to discover that Rod had been thinking about my future far more seriously than I ever had.

Yes, that fall, he asked me to marry him once I'd graduated. For me, the proposal came as quite the surprise. In retrospect, keeping all this from my father was undeniably an unwise decision, when I definitely could have used his guidance and mature perspective. Rod explained how we could live with his parents for a year while we had our own home built. To give him credit, he had everything planned. I kept his proposal secret, saying I needed time to think about it. In my relative innocence, I didn't fully understand all that he was offering me from a long-term, adult perspective. He was a good man looking for a life partner, a woman with whom to create a life, to start a family. I was a kid thinking about all the fun I would miss being stuck on a farm away from my city friends. Good grief, I didn't even drive a car!

This kind, caring man and I were not meant to share the same life journey. Our close friendship faded as time and distance drew us further apart, but we never totally lost touch as our families were so intertwined. Rod was my first love, with and within me since our parting, through all the subsequent years, destined to be in my heart forever. Upon receiving the unexpected letter about his being in palliative care, instantly, I knew I had to go.

I made the 220 km drive to the hospital to reunite with the man I hadn't seen in years, the first of thirteen visits I would make in just over fourteen weeks. I put on my happy face when I first entered his room, but my heart was breaking for this gentle, amazing man who had always loved me, the friend who would soon leave this world. His sister was with him when I arrived, sitting in a large brown recliner positioned to view both her brother and the doorway. I felt so grateful for her reaching out to me. Through the massive windows, sunlight beamed into the room, giving her an angelic appearance as it cascaded across her shoulders. The room was bright and inviting, as were their smiles.

Sitting in bed propped up by several pillows, Rod looked so frail, like a wee bird enfolded in a swirl of white hospital bedding. He was but a shadow of the man I last remembered seeing. Oh, how could this be? The body that had once been so strong was now challenging to hug because it caused him great pain. How could I bring him some joy in his final days? Knowing that sometimes all a person needs is a caring hand to hold, I held tight. I promised to return with my treasure of old photos and more stories to share. We reminisced about the happy times, the sad times in our lives, and the mutual knowing and understanding brought comfort to us both. When we first met officially, I was a foolish fifteen-year-old; he was eleven years my senior. Although he'd declared we should be married, I left him behind. He never married anyone else. While he was still able to speak, he sadly told me something my heart already knew. *"I would have given you a good life."*

Through the following weeks, Rod did his best to be positive and cheerful, while I watched his life slowly slipping away. Knowing the end was near, when I went for what would be our last Sunday visit, I brought a bottle of holy water from Ireland's famous Knock Shrine. I asked Rod for permission to bless him with the sacred water, and he agreed. I'm not sure if he genuinely believed in the gesture or simply thought it would make me feel better, but there was no denying that, in the moment of the anointment, we both felt at peace. Wanting clarity during his illness, Rod had refused most medication despite his significant discomfort. Seeing him fade away, enduring his physical misery brought to mind the biblical verse, *"Suffer little children to come unto me."* That evening, I prayed that God would keep him from the pain.

The call came on Thursday morning. If I wanted to see my lifelong love one more time, I should travel quickly. My old truck making the trip in record time, I had the privilege of being with Rod in his final hours. His sister, at his side all night, had since left the hospital just before I arrived. I held his hand, telling him I was near. Except for laboured breathing, he was still. Suddenly he stirred and asked, *"Who are these people? I don't know them!"* I gently slid my arm under his neck and shoulder whispering, *"Don't be afraid; they're angles waiting to take you home."*

Rod relaxed and took his last two short breaths as he journeyed into the light. Oh, my! What was I to do? I moved my arm from under him and kissed his forehead. As I rang the bell for the nurse, I had a sudden thought that his hair was mussed up, and I should brush it. Without moving him, I combed the hair on top of his head and waited.

Losing Rod taught me that when we're in doubt or without the life experience to decide on an opportunity, we should seek the counsel of a wise elder. Had I shared his declaration of marriage with my father, my life certainly would have been different. In my youth, I had no idea how important this proposal could have been to my future.

With the best of intention, people make thoughtless comments like *"You should be over it by now."* or *"Time will heal your heart."* Grieve at your own pace; don't be rushed as you move forward. Dealing with loss is an individual experience. No one has the right to dictate to us how we should grieve. If you are a person of faith, your beliefs will comfort you with the promise of everlasting life. The person is gone from this earth but not forgotten. Know that your loved ones will live on through your memories and conversations until you meet again. To the end of time, they will always have a piece of your heart.

To wait until someone is dying before you reveal your heart and mind is hurtful to you both. Don't hold back; speak your truth. Don't let your ego stop you from expressing what needs to be said. Find the courage. When a person keeps crossing our life path, the Universe is working with intention. Pay attention to the lessons.

Thank you, Rod, for the gifts you've given me.

Wendy L. Yost

Wendy L. Yost blends spiritual and leadership principles to assist individuals and organizations in taking inspired action and generating desired results. Highlights from the university Leadership course Wendy has taught for over a decade can be found in her TEDx Talk on *The Benefits of Learning to Listen to Your Life*. Wendy has contributed chapters for five Best Selling books -- and is currently working on a Children's Book about trusting ourselves and our senses, including intuition. Woven throughout all that Wendy does is her passion for guiding students and clients toward more of what matters most to them.

You can reach Wendy at:
https://moreisavailable.com/
https://www.facebook.com/wendy.yost
https://www.linkedin.com/in/wendylyostmoreisavailble

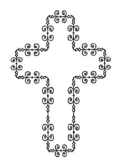

Chapter 9

Cultivating Love's Eternal Connection

By Wendy L. Yost

"Grief is praise, because it is the natural way love honors what it misses."

–Martín Prechtel

When I was growing up, my family had a cat named Licorice who lived to be 22 years old. Since that was my first experience with a house cat, that is how long I thought cats live. Which made it hard to face, as an adult, that my sweet boy Christofur, rescued through mystical circumstances, was going to need my help making his way from his current cat life into his next incarnation, after just seven years.

Christofur and I found one another following the difficult decision to end my marriage. After a year of focusing my attention on the seemingly relentless financial and emotional logistics involved with recovering from a divorce, I decided to invite love into my life again. With that in mind, I headed to the local Metaphysical Bookstore in search of a statue of Bast, the Egyptian Cat Goddess of Play, Pleasure and Sensuality, to add to an altar I was creating. Sure enough, they had exactly what I was looking for, but it happened to be on a shelf in a locked cabinet. As I headed to the office to ask for the key, my eyes landed on a photo essay of a very handsome cat, with the headline, "Looking for My Forever Home".

Up until that point, despite the well-intentioned promptings of several close friends, I had no interest in adding a pet to my life or my responsibilities. I was decidedly focused on re-learning how to take care of myself and taking my time in doing so. Yet the moment my eyes landed on Christofur's picture, the thought that came, accompanied by a huge heartfelt smile was, *"There you are!"* I asked for a copy of the photo essay, and with my Bast statue in hand, I headed to my car and called the number to see if he was still available. He was! And that night I went to a pet store to purchase everything I could possibly need to bring him home.

Christofur was so much more than a cat. He was an Abyssinian Siamese mix, who brought love and joy into every corner of my home, heart and life. Abyssinians were the cats assigned to protect Sacred Temples in Egypt, something I had always felt a kinship with. So between our meeting by way of Bast and his breed having an affiliation with Egypt, it felt like synchronicity had a hand in our meeting. And, it felt like we were together again, after having been separated.

I will forever hold dear Christofur's many trills and chirps, his tail swishes anytime I would lay down to enjoy an afternoon nap, and his being a post-it note "goalie" -- always interested in swatting any crumpled post-it notes I'd toss on the floor while going about my day. He was 13 pounds of masculine energy, protector of my home and expander of my heart. I got to explore new aspects of myself being his Kitty Mamma -- and I loved it! So when it came time to say goodbye, so much sooner than I had anticipated given my experience with my childhood pet, it was devastating.

Gratefully, I had heard of a service called Lap of Love Veterinary Hospice that will come to your home when a furry family member needs assistance bringing their life to an end. It was clear to me, based on a number of things I had observed and that had been observed by multiple veterinarians, that Christofur was no longer able to comfortably be a cat. On Easter Sunday, things had gotten to the point where he couldn't jump up on all of the surfaces he surfed so easily in the past, his appetite was lessening, and his once youthful and vocal ways had dimmed and quieted greatly. He was in pain. And I was afraid every time I left the house that something awful would happen.

After several weeks and numerous vet visits, I remember deciding to have a conversation with Christofur directly. I asked him what he needed, asked if he needed my help dying, prayed over his answers and then made the call to Lap of Love. Within two hours, one of the most compassionate human beings I have ever met in my life arrived, Dr. Tina Olivieri. She assessed Christofur's current state and agreed, that while there is no right time, there is a window of time where you can guarantee a peaceful passing, take your time saying your goodbyes and most importantly, relieve any suffering being experienced. So that is what I did.

Having seen countless tributes to pets who have passed posted to social media through the years, I knew that I was not ready that night or even that week, to share anything that publicly. Instead, after Dr. Tina departed, I envisioned a circle of love around me, people who knew me well *and* who had special relationships of their own with Christofur. I sent each person who came to mind a text, letting them know that Christofur had completed his life as a cat -- and thanking them for loving him, and me, so well. I then drove to my parent's house, to spend the night there, so that when I woke up the first morning without Christofur's physical presence, I would be supported in managing the emotions sure to arise.

Experiencing something familiar, in a way other than we've grown accustomed to experiencing it, can be incredibly jarring. And that was the new reality I found myself in, as I would forget that Christofur had passed and then get catapulted into remembering, each time I did something out of habit, in some way related to him, after he passed. I quickly realized how many of my routines were designed with Christofur in mind, not to mention the countless belongings I had purchased for him over the years that shouted his absence to me each time my eyes landed on them.

After about 24 hours of this, I decided I needed a different way to handle all of the things I was noticing as suddenly absent or no longer necessary. I decided to start a specific journal just for this purpose. Each time I did something out of habit that I no longer needed to do the way I had become accustomed to doing it (like checking to make sure the door was closed behind me when I went to get my mail), I noted it in my journal. As the days turned to weeks, some relief set in. In place of what initially brought sadness, noticing these things started to bring gratitude, for the many ways that I loved Christofur and that he showed his love for me. The journal, and all of the details recorded in it, has since become a treasured keepsake.

Other adjustments were also necessary. I missed hearing the sound of his trills and chirps filling the house. And while I had captured several on video that I could watch if desired, my townhouse was now undeniably quiet. One day it occurred to me to put the "Cat Calm" CD I had purchased to play for Christofur when I left the house to new use, for me. While it felt a little silly at the time, I left the CD on constant repeat and it helped a lot in having the house feel less quiet and empty when I came home each day. I also deeply missed the sweet tail swish of his that always accompanied our afternoon naps. So at a local store I scanned a selection of super soft blankets and picked one out that mimicked his grey and white coloring. That $20 purchase of tangible solace continues to bring me comfort each time my eyes land on it or I tuck myself under it.

In the months that followed Christofur's passing, I sought professional help in a variety of ways: Attending a workshop called, *Reconnecting with Your Life After Loss,* facilitated by Grief Counselor, Maryann Udel; attending a Pet Parent Grief Support Group led by Veterinarian and Compassion Fatigue Expert, Dr. Kathleen Ayl; consulting with a dear friend, Mark Mezadourian, a gifted Intuitive and Medium; and purchasing an Oracle Deck to use specifically for conversations I wanted to have with Christofur. Each of these action steps helped me feel less alone and more supported, as I continued to find my footing in this new reality. Though I knew I could talk to family and friends, I found that I was willing to share more of what I was experiencing in communities with others who were grieving – or by being assisted by those specifically trained to help people move through grief.

Through my work with these professionals, I was able to see that some of what I was experiencing wasn't limited to the loss of Christofur, and that it included the loss of my marriage, and what I thought my life would be like prior to determining the need for a divorce. When this was gently illuminated, something that took place at a workshop I participated in shortly after ending my marriage readily came to mind. At the start of it, the facilitators asked each person in attendance to share their name and where they were in their divorce process. The woman next to me shared that she was divorced in 1971. I am sure my face reacted as I realized that she had been divorced as long as I had been alive. Truth be told, in the moment, I was pretty quick to judge her for not having "gotten over it" nearly four decades later. Yet as the workshop went on, she shared that she had had a good life, yet as she approached her retirement, sadness remained over the life she once thought she would be living at this point.

That woman gave me a gift. Through what she shared, I realized that when we lose someone we love, grief arrives on two tracks: The immediate experience of the loss of their physical presence and all that accompanies it -- and what we thought the future would look, feel and be like with them in our life. Both tracks need tending to in different ways and at different times. And the woman at the workshop helped me to see that it would serve me well to consider how to best go about doing so when it came to Christopher's passing. For me, that meant giving nearly all of Christofur's belongings to an organization that fosters cats until they find their forever homes. It was a way of completing the circle of how Christofur and I came to meet one another, while putting to use the items we gathered on our shared path in ways that would support other families on theirs. It also allowed me the freedom to recreate my home in new ways. Aware that, had I held on to more of his belongings, would have involved lesser changes.

Now when something happens that moves me into the territory of grief, I feel differently equipped. Instead of old upsets resurfacing and compounding as new upsets make their way into my life, it's as if I am walking up a spiral staircase and with each turn of the spiral, I can see something similar, yet who I am, how I see it, and what I bring to my seeing it has evolved as a result of how I chose to care for myself following Christofur's passing. And as a result, I can choose to meet new circumstances I find myself in, in new ways.

I knew something significant had shifted within me when I found myself having a conversation with Christofur, while driving a canyon in my area, well after he passed. There was no sadness, just this moment of pure joy, sunroof open, windows down, birds chirping, breeze on my face – and my thinking, *Christofur would love everything about this moment!* And realizing that there was nothing hindering that from being so. I no longer had to work to keep him safely at home in the townhouse. He could join me anywhere, anytime. His spirit was along for the ride, unbound by a body that had done what it could for as long as it could -- and I couldn't help but smile over my capacity to simply enjoy the moment with him.

September 10th will mark the ninth anniversary of Christofur and I reconnecting in this life, in the ways that we did. And this coming Easter will be the two-year anniversary of his passing. I've learned from sharing in both his life and his death that our loved ones walk beside us always, just differently once they've passed. And that while what I've done to move through the grief that accompanied Christofur's passing may not make sense to anyone else, it has assisted me greatly – and it still makes me incredibly happy to crumple up post-it notes and toss them about the house in honor of him and the love we share.

Conclusion

"Death is only the beginning to a whole new journey we are yet to experience"

~ Kate Batten

I hope by reading the stories in this book it has helped you on your own journey. I hope it has provided you with a ray of light to give you hope that the sun will shine again in your heart. You will smile, you will laugh again, and your grief will change form as time goes on.

I learned on my own journey of grief that we do not just morn people when they die, but we also morn many other things too. Things like broken relationships, the loss of pets, and lost experiences from our past. Yet, no matter the experience that caused the grief in the first place, there is always 5 stages of grief we walk through.

Those 5 stages are:

- Denial.
- Anger.
- Bargaining.
- Depression.
- Acceptance.

These 5 stages can take weeks, months, years or even decades to work through. It all depends on the person and the experience. I would encourage you to study these 5 stages and see where you are on your own journey. When I studied these 5 stages, it did give me greater understanding of my own loss, and it may help you too.

I want to thank you so much for purchasing and reading *The Missing Piece, Coping with Grief*. If you have enjoyed this book and would like to reach out to me, then please do!

God Bless You!

Kate ☺

www.instagram.com/kate_batten

The Missing Piece

The Missing Piece book series is an international bestselling book series compiled and authored by Kate Batten.

What first started out as an empowerment Facebook page for victims of domestic violence quickly grew into an internationally published book series. The Missing Piece book series has helped touch thousands of people's lives across the world by helping others share their stories.

If you would like to reach out to Kate, or follow her work, you can at: www.instagram.com/kate_batten

Printed by Amazon Italia Logistica S.r.l.
Torrazza Piemonte (TO), Italy

41996643R00085